FOLLOWING
THE
Whispers

FOLLOWING

THE

Whispers

*Creating a life of inner peace and self-acceptance
from the depths of despair*

KAREN WALKER

Author's Note

Out of respect for their privacy, I have changed the names of some people who appear in these pages, but all the events and the people described are true as I remember them and as they happened according to my perspective.

Acknowledgements

It would not have been possible for me to complete this project without the love and support of many others. First, my son, David, for nodding his permission to write this story; my husband, Gary, whose unconditional love created the environment for me to write and whose financial support gave me the freedom to do so; my first editor, Dina Wolff, who showed me how to give shape and form to all the parts of my life and whose expert editing skills and loving guidance brought me through the painful, yet cathartic process of writing; Clara, who encouraged me to publish the first essay I ever wrote; Mary Alice, my Guardian Angel; the Creative Writing professors at the University of New Mexico's English Department, especially Greg Martin, Marissa Clark, Lisa Chavez and Jack Trujillo, who showed me how to "tell my story;" all the folks at Bascom Hill Publishing Group for making this happen; a special thanks to Mark R., who started me on the road to recovery; Dr. Barbara Newman and Becky Bosch, who helped me unfreeze enough to begin writing again. And to my readers—Clara A., Linda R., Gayle V., Wendy B., Karen V. and Steve W.—your willingness to provide loving feedback and support from the earliest stages helped keep me going. Thank you.

Introduction

John Lennon was right when he said, *"Living is easy with eyes closed, misunderstanding all you see."* Like ostriches, we plunk our heads down and pretend everything is okay—because if we lift our heads up and take a peek around, we might have to make difficult, painful choices that could hurt, disappoint, or anger someone else as well as ourselves. Or we might deny or ignore what we feel because we don't have a solution to the dilemma we are facing. In order to remain silent in a situation we know is wrong, however, we have to silence the parts of us that know better.

I don't know when I stopped paying attention. It could have been after the sexual abuse occurred at six years old. Or maybe even before that, when I cowered in my room trying to block out the screaming matches between my parents. My home life, along with events for which I had neither the knowledge nor the skills to handle well, created a self-hatred so unbearable, I shut down. We cannot possibly hear guidance of any kind when we are numb, so the first twenty-eight years of my life were lived unconsciously, with devastating consequences. At that point, at twenty-eight years old, I lost custody of my only child. Until then I'd been sleepwalking through my life but didn't know it.

In the 1970's women rarely lost custody, unless they were prostitutes or drug addicts or something of that nature. I was none of the above. I am a nice Jewish girl from a white, middle class neighborhood in Queens, NY. My father was a clerk in the United States Post Office, and my

1

mother sold real estate. My parents weren't alcoholic. I didn't drop out of school. I had friends.

Underneath the depression/despair cycle that permeated my existence burned a question I couldn't answer: what was wrong with me that I ended up losing my child?

Paradoxically, that same tragedy put me on the path towards healing. Seeping out from the blanket of depression which cloaked me were long-buried memories, thoughts, and feelings from childhood. I began to keep a journal. I didn't know it then, but journaling gave me a way to unscramble the pieces of my life so that I could begin to make sense of it. That, along with private therapy, self-help groups, women's consciousness raising groups, self-help books, and talking with friends, provided tools I needed to answer my soul-searing question.

Following the Whispers is a chronicle of that journey. It illustrates the consequences of not listening to the voice of wisdom and shows how I learned to tune in to and trust that inner voice. Now, at fifty-nine, I am aware of messages trying to get through. It might be a sensation in my body—sometimes in my gut, sometimes in my chest—or a thought such as *this doesn't feel right* or *something's wrong here*. The thought can be so fleeting I question whether it was really there.

I've learned to distinguish the thoughts or sensations that were confusing as a child. There is a parent voice—*don't have sex before you're married*. Other times, the voice of my conscience speaks up—*that's wrong, don't do it*. My child voice clamors for attention as well—*I want that piece of chocolate now, please don't hurt me, I can't or won't do that*. Then there is my intuition, a guidance that helps me know what I am feeling—*what that person said was derogatory and hurtful, no wonder I am upset*. And more and more frequently, there is a wise, logical adult voice to help me make informed decisions—*if you purchase that item, your budget for next month will be shot*. There is yet another voice—one I've come to call Spirit—that whispers in a language of non-words—a gentle nudge that makes me stop, pause, and breathe before taking an action.

Today I am content, although I still work on changing the things I can and accepting the things I cannot. My search for answers taught me that inner peace is not something we achieve and then remain feeling that way forever. It comes in moments. My spiritual journey towards healing has been and continues to be eclectic and varied and no doubt

2

differs from yours, but it is my deepest hope that whatever might be keeping you from feeling inner peace and contentment, you will find pieces of my story to relate to and inspiration to move forward in your own journey towards healing.

Karen Walker, summer, 2008

The more faithfully you listen to the voices within you, the better you will hear what is sounding outside.

Dag Hammarskjold

Chapter 1

In The Beginning...
There Was Self-Hatred

My friend Chuck waltzes around the room, his nine-year-old daughter, Sivan, snuggled in his right arm, her six-year-old sister, Amali, nestled in his left. The two girls' arms are wrapped around each other behind their dad's neck, and their giggles can be heard from where I sit on the other side of the large dance studio, where our community of folk dancers gathers every Saturday night. Watching this man with his children, I can't help thinking how lucky these two little girls are and how different their childhood is from mine.

Childhood should be a sanctuary—a refuge before the onslaught of life—a cocoon in which one feels unconditionally loved. This prepares us for hardship. It provides a foundation upon which we can grow; a strength in the knowledge that whatever challenges we might face, the foundation will hold us up.

My childhood was no such thing. Nor was my home a place where I felt safe, secure, or loved. There were moments of sanctuary, alone in my room, tucked behind the closed door listening to records and singing. But the sound of my parents' fighting overshadowed the soothing sound of the music—and the coldness between my parents seeped under the door and crept into my room, filling it and me with the lack of love that chilled our house.

I found sanctuary for a brief moment with Louis when I was sixteen

4

and in love for the first time. He was eighteen and already in college. As Orthodox Jews, his family kept the Sabbath, which meant not turning on a light, cooking, listening to the radio, watching television, or riding. Saturday was spent in synagogue. Upon coming home, the family ate together, and then read quietly, having left the light on the night before. During the prayers that were said at each meal, I could feel the love flowing through the home in the words and actions of this mother and father. That sanctuary ended though, sometime after my Senior Prom, when Louis lied to me about his compulsive gambling and about dating a girl named Fern.

When I finally found sanctuary I was forty-six, unlike Sivan and Amali, who are growing up in the very heart of it—receiving both a father and mother's unconditional support in a home where love lives.

Once in awhile, Sivan has a sleepover at our house. As Gary slips her upside down and runs from room to room with Buddy, our blue heeler chasing after them, Sivan's laughter fills our home. She and I sing along as we watch *Oklahoma* together and my heart bursts with joy. Sivan calls us her "pretend grandparents" and says she loves us just the same as her "real" ones. My life now is sanctuary. But to find out how I got here, we must travel back in time to my childhood to discover where, when, and how I learned to hate myself.

* * *

For as long as I can remember, a lead ball lived in my chest and a whirling dervish resided in my stomach—sensations I now call anxiety—but as a child, it was all I knew and so it was normal. These sensations were so uncomfortable and pervasive, I wanted to disappear from my own body and become someone else. At first, I didn't have words for these feelings. But as I grew older, the long list of how I longed to be different began: blonde hair instead of black; straight, not curly; wanting to belong to another family—feeling like an alien in my own; being 5'3 ½", not 5'7; crooked yellow teeth, not straight white ones; freckles covering my face instead of clear, flawless skin. The list of character traits I had that I didn't want would fill an entire journal.

We aren't born hating ourselves. Those feelings grow as we grow, from the early ways we are nurtured (or not), through beliefs and assumptions

5

we make about ourselves from interactions with parents, other family members, teachers, friends and strangers. Early on, I learned to distrust my own perceptions, discounting them to such an extent that it became impossible to separate what I thought and felt from what others thought and felt. I had no center—no core sense of who I was.

I was born in 1949 in the Bronx, one of five boroughs that comprise the city of New York. Five days later, we moved to a small apartment in Jackson Heights, a multi-ethnic neighborhood in Queens (another of the boroughs), where I spent the rest of my childhood. Dad was thirty-three when I arrived on the scene, and he worked at a local pizza parlor. Pictures of him reveal a slim, dark-haired man with a thin face and a mischievous smile. Mom was thirty at the time of my birth and stayed home with me those first few years. She had brown, wavy hair, light, sea-green eyes, and a near-perfect figure.

"A goddess," Dad would say when we looked at old photos together years later.

Both of them were born and raised in New York. My father's mom died when Dad was only seven. His nine-year-old brother was sent to an orphanage, while my father lived with his granddad till he turned nine. At that point, Dad went to the orphanage as well.

At fifteen, Dad ran away from "the home" as he called it, and did what many others did back then—rode the rails. During the Depression, there wasn't enough money to feed entire families, so one or two members would leave. Homeless, out of work and hungry, they were called hoboes, living hand-to-mouth, begging for food, and hopping freight trains to get from one town to the next. For the next four years of his life, my dad lived the life of a hobo, something for which he seemed deeply ashamed.

In 1941, at twenty-seven, he lied about his education (he had only finished eight grade) and joined the Army. When he was sent overseas to North Africa, he participated in one of the invasions that preceded D-Day in Normandy. On the third day in Africa, Dad watched two buddies die directly in front of him. The shrapnel from one of the shells hit Dad. That wound won him a Purple Heart and a ticket home. My father's time in the Army is the only period in his life he talked about with sincere pride. A short time after his discharge, he met my mother. From photos, I can see why they fell for each other and married so quickly—within three months of meeting each other. They were a handsome couple. I came along three years later, but Dad's childhood had left him ill-prepared for marriage and family life.

Mom's early years sheds some light onto why she, too, had a difficult time with marriage and childcare. During her birth, an instrument touched a nerve. This somehow created Parkinson's disease-like symptoms which caused her hands to shake, a physical affliction that made life difficult. In school, kids made fun of her. It was hard for her to hold a glass, take a drink, or put make-up on. Her writing was nearly illegible and doing any kind of manual task posed a challenge. She did, however, manage to graduate high school, and worked as a hat model until she married Dad.

Throughout her life, my mother's family tried to convince her she was too handicapped to lead a normal life. Don't drive, don't marry, and don't have children, she was told. In fact, one story I remember was about Olga, one of my mother's aunts. Convinced my mother wasn't capable of raising a baby, Olga unsuccessfully tried to adopt me away from my parents. Mom seemed furious as she related this story. From the way she spoke about her family, I gathered she ignored their opinions and pretty much did what she wanted. But I suspect that underneath my mother's bravado lurked a vulnerable and insecure young girl—one who became a woman determined never to let anyone see the hurt inside.

Put these two damaged souls together and it is like throwing unidentified chemicals into a pot. Add a baby to the mix, with its own chemical configuration, and explosions are sure to occur. Neither of my parents dealt with tough situations nor challenging feelings in a healthy manner. They had never learned how. It follows, therefore, that they did not have the skills or knowledge to teach a child how to navigate life skillfully. Unlike many of my friends, I was not taught values, ethics, or indeed, how to solve problems. If I strayed off course, I was given no guidance, no compass, no gentle words of wisdom. As an only child, I lived in the war zone my parents created with their constant battles. I felt like I imagine a young, inadequately trained soldier might feel negotiating land littered with minefields, cut off from the commanders in charge. She hears faulty radio equipment emitting mostly static with perhaps a word or two coming through, which the young soldier attempts to interpret. Out in the field, alone and without resources, she is totally dependent on her own feelings and perceptions. When anxiety is the

7

guiding principle one lives by, perceptions are sure to be inaccurate. When I did make decisions on my own, it was often with dire consequences. It wouldn't be until I found the twelve-step programs some twenty years later that I started learning principles to live by that helped me make better choices.

* * *

"I don't want to go to sleep, I'm not tired," I whined.

"It's your bedtime and we'll have no arguments," my mother commanded. "Go to your room and get into bed—now!"

"No."

"I said now!"

"No."

"All right, young lady, you'll see what happens when you don't listen."

Most of my childhood is a blur, but I imagine this is pretty close to what must have gone on between my mother and me one night back in 1952, when I was little more than three years old. I'll never forget the large, semi-circular green chair that stood in the corner of our living room. It had flat, beige leather arms and thick velvet cushions and I loved curling up in it, listening to books being read to me. At least I did before my mother used it to punish me.

Years later, I heard the story. After I refused to go to bed, Mom forced me into that big green chair and told me to stay. If I started to fall asleep, she slapped me across the face to wake me up. This went on all night long.

"You never resisted going to sleep at bedtime again," Mom would say when she retold that story, quite proud of her parenting skills. I don't remember being particularly shocked or even thinking there was anything wrong with what she had done. I'd just assumed all mothers disciplined that way. Today, I see this as child abuse.

Mom's way of handling my toddler rebellion did, indeed, keep me from disobeying, but it also broke my spirit. At such an early age, it was impossible to speak up for myself, so I learned to be a good little girl who understood not to cry when I wanted something, not to ask for things, and to always follow the rules. Confronting people terrified me. Convinced my own needs did not matter, I kept them hidden to preserve

8

peace. Therapists later explained that this incident was the root of my adult issues—that my mother had actually tortured me.

We know now from studies on childhood development, that children require some degree of nurturing to grow up with enough self-esteem and confidence to thrive in this world. Unfortunately, my parents, along with other parents in the 1950's, did not know this. I grew up feeling love was conditional, dependent on how I behaved or what I said or didn't say. The basis of the love shifted like quicksand, so I never knew what I needed to do or say to achieve the love and acceptance I craved and every child so desperately requires.

One night, when I was six or seven, I woke up and wandered into the living room. My mother was sitting at the foot of a chair while Charlie, a single man and neighbor of ours, sat in the chair with his hands on my mother's hair and shoulders. My father was at work. A feeling in my gut whispered something wasn't right. I don't remember what I said to my mother that night, but I was called a liar and made to believe I didn't see what I saw. I know now that I have a powerful intuitive voice, but from incidents like this, I learned that giving voice to those feelings got me in trouble. Either I was made to feel wrong, called a liar, or my words got twisted so I felt confused and unsure of what I wanted to say. My voice was silenced. Because my family denied my reality, I learned to deny it as well. Soon I stopped listening to that inner guidance and eventually forgot it was even there.

* * *

"Mom, Dad, can we light Chanukah candles?" I asked breathlessly. I'd been across the street at my friend, Betty's, where they'd just lit theirs.

"What do you want to do that for?" Dad asked. We were Jewish, but my parents' were agnostics. Unlike most of my friends, I'd never attended synagogue services or Hebrew School.

"Because we're supposed to," I said.

"We don't do that," Mom said. "It's ridiculous."

"But, but…" I sputtered.

"If you want to waste your time, go right ahead," said Dad. "We won't stop you."

9

I proceeded to put the pretty multi-colored candles in the silver holder Betty's mother had loaned me. She'd called it a menorah. On the back of the candle box, a prayer was written in Hebrew and spelled out phonetically in English. Slowly, I said the prayer out loud as I lit the candles, not understanding a single word. But a sense of peace slipped over me—a feeling I would seek to find again and again as I grew up. For those few moments, my parents' fights didn't touch me, my stomach didn't hurt, and calmness radiated from inside me. I began to attend synagogue services with Betty and her family on Jewish holidays. Although the language was foreign, the rituals and ceremonies resonated within me. Thus the seed was planted for the spiritual journey I would embark upon some twenty years later.

Wanting to participate in Judaism was one of many ways I felt different from my parents. This separateness led to feeling alone, ugly, stupid, and no good—a litany of self talk which grew increasingly more damaging as the years went on. As an adult, my mother shared that when I was quite small, my father used to sit me on his lap and say, "You're ugly."

Later on, my father confessed that he used to tell me, "You're no good," and I would say back, "I'm good for you." He didn't seem to recognize how hurtful this must have been to a small child; he had no remorse at that time.

It wasn't all bad, though. On Sundays we'd make the forty-five minute trip from Queens across the Triborough Bridge to the Bronx to visit my grandmother. Most of the time, my cousins, Richard and Joyce, would meet us there and we'd play dominoes, build houses with decks of cards and spend time in the park across the street. Grandma made my favorite foods, a Hungarian dish called cabbage noodles, and chicken noodle soup with matzo balls. While Uncle Freddie and Dad watched ballgames in the living room, Aunt Charlotte and Mom sat around the kitchen table watching Grandma fuss at the stove. Despite the small spats and disagreements that seemed to be the lifeblood of these particular Hungarians, there was a loving energy as well while sharing meals and playing with my cousins.

There was one particular character trait I developed as a result of my childhood that I share with children who grew up in alcoholic homes—blaming myself for my parents' problems. Moreover, I believed it was my job to fix them. Like the time I found Mom sitting on the couch, her hands shaking more than usual, her face scrunched up. She stared at the floor.

"Mom, what's wrong?" I asked, kneeling in front of her. I must have been seven or eight years old.

"Nothing, Karen," she said.

But I knew something was up, and kept asking until she told me what happened.

"Your father threw a hanger at me," she said. "I told him to get out."

"Is he coming back?" I asked.

"I don't know and I don't care."

"Please, Mommy, can't we call and tell him to come home? It will be all right. You'll see," I said, doing what had become habit—trying to make my mother feel better. What Mom hadn't bothered to tell me was how she'd probably instigated the hanger throwing in the first place. Locked in an intricate battle dance, my parents took turns baiting one another. As time went on, my mother would throw this incident back in my face when she complained about how miserable she was with my father, implying it was my fault because I made her get my father to come back home.

Looking back on this exchange, what strikes me most is the role reversal. A young child should not be placed in the position of parenting her own parents. But it devastated me that they were both miserable, so I took on the task of making them happy. This, of course, only led to feelings of inadequacy, since there was nothing I could do to relieve their suffering. What also strikes me is how I used intuition to determine what my mom was thinking and feeling, but did not use the skill for myself. I can see now that I was simply trying to control my environment to the best of my ability—to keep the peace at all costs—even if that meant losing my own identity.

If I close my eyes, I can see my family a few years later. We had moved from a six-story garden apartment to a two-family house in which we rented the upstairs apartment. Our living room was dominated by an entertainment center containing a stereo and TV. The furniture was crushed velvet; the carpet yellow-green shag. In the dining room was a small, round, brown Formica table with four chairs. On the wall behind it was a mural with a Japanese floral design in varying shades of beige. Mom sits in her chair in the living room, chain smoking, her right leg crossed over her left. A stern expression graces her face; one might even call it cold. Because she didn't show emotion, it was impossible to gauge her moods. What I remember is a nervous, agitated mother, emotionally smothering one minute, distant the next, blaming Dad and me for what was wrong in her life. The only time I saw Mom smile was when she was with her friends, playing Mah Jongg or Canasta.

In this imagined scene, Dad and I are watching baseball together, me leaning up against him on the couch. My grandparents lived diagonally across the street from Yankee Stadium in the Bronx and Dad and I spent many a Saturday and Sunday afternoon watching Mickey Mantle, Roger Maris, Yogi Bera and the rest of the Bronx Bombers blast their way to World Series wins.

Dad didn't speak—he bellowed. With his harsh, gruff voice, he appeared angry and resentful a good deal of the time. Black rages would explode from him, seeming to spring out of nowhere, and he would scream obscenities at Mom and me. I felt like the rope in a tug of war between them—one minute on Mom's side, the next on Dad's, living in fear that the frayed rope would break one day and I'd be split apart. That fear ruled my choices and my behavior for many years, until I learned to bring it out of the darkness of my unconscious and into the light of awareness.

Every few years we moved, each new home located only a few miles from the last one, which meant adjusting to a new apartment, new teachers, and new classmates, as well as making new friends. Moving so frequently made no sense to me—my father held the same job at the same location for the U.S. Postal Service for many years. My guess is the rent would be raised and my parents, having grown up during the Depression, wanted to save money. Unfortunately, they weren't aware that frequently disrupting a child's structure could create insecure feelings. I had no stable foundation upon which to build a healthy life. Battling parents and an already crushed spirit made it virtually impossible for me to forge a sense of self. What happened instead was lessons in how to become a woman out of touch with herself—a woman who operated like a plane on auto-pilot. Just push the right button and I'd alter course or turn right or left.

My childhood took place in the 1950's, when television first entered American homes. In our house, the only time we weren't watching TV was when we were sleeping. I raced home from school to watch Annette Funicello and Tim Considine, Bobby and the rest of the gang on "The Mickey Mouse Club." Immediately after that, Dick Clark's "American Bandstand" came on and I'd wish I could dance with Charlie, the kid who seemed to have rubber legs. Evenings were spent watching "Father Knows Best," "Leave it to Beaver," "Bonanza," and "My Three Sons." Here were families I longed to be part of. *When I have my own family*, I vowed, *things will be different.*

Chapter 2

The Painter

"*When you wish upon a star, makes no difference who you are, anything your heart desires will come to you.*" Jiminy Cricket was mistaken when he sang this song to Pinocchio, although in the fairy tale, Pinocchio's wish to become a real boy came true. Not so in real life, however.

I can remember standing outside as a small child. When Venus first poked through the velvety blackness of the night sky, I couldn't resist closing my eyes, crossing my fingers and silently saying, "*Starlight, Star Bright, first star I see tonight, wish I may, wish I might, make this wish come true tonight.*" My wishes were that my parents would stop fighting; that mommy would smile; that I knew what my teacher was talking about. I wished I belonged to another family. I don't know when I first heard the term, "*That's wishful thinking,*" but at some point, I learned that we don't get what we wish for. So I stopped dreaming. It wasn't until I was in my fifties that I understood it is okay to want things—but you must also understand that you might not get everything you want.

* * *

I was a pawn my parents' used to fuel their arguments. Being an only child, I had no siblings to diffuse the negative energy directed towards me. One good thing about being the only child, however, was having

14

my own room. It was a sanctuary of sorts in a child's world filled with anxiety and fear. For hours I'd remain engrossed in music I played on my small victrola (a record player). My parents' had Frank Sinatra, Sarah Vaughn, Duke Ellington, Glenn Miller, Doris Day, and more, and I was singing "Witchcraft," "Secret Love", and "Cheek to Cheek" by the time I was seven. Patsy Cline crooning "Crazy" would drown out my parents' loud voices in the living room. When I sang along with Patsy or the Everly Brothers, or even Elvis, I forgot everything else. At four, I began taking ballet and tap dancing lessons, one of the few bright spots in my life. But at seven, that joy went away, and all I knew was that I was a lonely little girl, hungry for love and comfort. And by the time I turned eight, I knew I'd never find that love and nurturing inside my own home.

* * *

"I want to go out and play now," I said.

"Why don't you change out of your new dress?" Mom asked. We had just come home from visiting Grandma in the Bronx.

"I'll be careful, I promise," I said, running out of my room and down the three flights of stairs. On the ground floor, a door stood open to one of the apartments and a man was inside, painting. Leaning against the doorframe, I was mesmerized by brush strokes spreading white paint over pale pink walls.

The man turned to me and asked, "Do you want to help?"

"Sure," I said, walking over to where he stood next to the closet, a big bucket of paint at his feet. He lifted me onto a ladder, handed me a brush and told me to paint the closet shelf.

I became lost in a world of white; the smell of paint mixed with something like Daddy's Old Spice, but deeper, earthier, like wet dirt. The painter stood behind me as I moved the brush back and forth, sheltered in the circle of his arms while he painted along with me. His white overalls were streaked with dirt and paint. They were baggy and hid the hard thing poking my back. After a bit, he put the paintbrush down and shifted his hand from the closet shelf to my chest, rubbing back and forth. Slowly, he lifted my dress, his fingers probing on top of my underpants, while that hard thing nudged between my legs. His fingers slipped inside my

15

panties and I leaned back, enjoying a tingling sensation. But my tummy started to hurt and pretty soon my "down there" got sore. *Stop*, I wanted to say. But I couldn't. His fingers were rough and chapped. His mouth nibbled my ear. Paint dripped into my hair and onto the sleeve of my pretty new dress. *Oh no, Mom's gonna kill me.*

My mind drifted as paint covered dirt on the closet shelf. *Almost done—just that small spot in the corner and I can go. But it feels so good, but I better go. But. But. But. Hurry up and finish. Hurry up and finish. There. All done.*

"I have to go now."

"Okay, but listen. Don't tell anyone you helped me. It will be our little secret. Understand?"

The look in the painter's eyes conveyed something different than the gentleness of his voice. This would not be the last time men gave me mixed messages, saying one thing with their words and another with their tone, gesture and actions.

"Yes, I understand."

I stepped down from the ladder and ran upstairs. As I pulled the dress over my head, Mom walked in. Sometimes I thought Mom was a witch—she seemed to know things without being told. "What's going on?" she asked.

"Nothing, Mom. Nothing." I heard her voice inside my head saying she would know if I ever lied to her. But the painter had said not to tell anyone.

Mom walked over and put her hands through my black hair.

"What's this, Karen? It looks like paint. Where did this come from?"

"I don't know," I said. But there was no stopping her. She kept at me until I told her about the painter; how he called me in and said I could help.

"Did he do anything? What happened?" She shook me, hysterical. I don't remember much after this point. Today, I understand how frightened Mom must have been, but back then it came across as anger. This exchange with my mother was one of the earliest times in my life where I misinterpreted someone's words and behavior. I thought she was angry that I got paint on my new dress. I was afraid the painter would be angry that I told. Much later in my life, I was grateful for my mother's sixth sense. But in that moment, confusion reigned. Why was she so

16

upset? Something was wrong, but I had no idea what. That confusion led to drawing erroneous conclusions—like it was my fault the painter did what he had done, and that feeling good was wrong. As I grew up, a similar pattern repeated itself. If I was involved in a discussion or argument and had conflicting feelings and the other person was upset, I would get quiet rather than speak up or ask for clarification. Then I would invariably make inaccurate assumptions about what the other person was feeling as well as what their intentions were.

I told Mom how the painter put me on a ladder and touched me down there, feeling me all over. She ran out of the room, leaving me standing there, alone. A neighbor kept the painter occupied while Mom called the police. Dad had already left for his night job at the Post Office. Time blurred as I stood frozen in my room, arms stiff at my sides, knees locked tight, my tummy aching.

Eventually two male detectives arrived and brought us to the police station, where I was led into a room without my mom. Surrounded by adult males, I repeated what I had told my mother.

"Do you know the difference between truth and lying?" they asked.

"Yes. I'm not lying," I cried. If there were other questions, I don't remember.

Over the next few months, Mom and Dad periodically removed me from school so I could testify in court. I don't remember what was said. What I do remember is feeling small. The room was cavernous; the judge sat high and imposing. The trial was postponed repeatedly and one time Mom considered dropping the charges because I became so distraught. I didn't want to leave school, didn't like court, didn't want to go, didn't want to answer any more questions, and I didn't want to see the painter's wife sitting there holding her baby. What I *did* want was food—comfort items like tuna fish and macaroni and cheese—but I especially wanted chocolate. There were always sweets in our house, and the day of the painter, when we got home from the police station, I discovered the numbing benefit of eating. That afternoon several chocolate cupcakes seemed to soothe the discomfort in my gut. It was the first time I used food to cover emotional pain, an act which would one day become compulsive. Geneen Roth, in *When Food is Love*, says that as children, some of us have no power to make choices about our situations. If we feel the pain around us is too intense and we can't leave or change it, we choose to shut it off. We will—and do—switch our pain to something less threatening: a compulsion.

It would be twenty years before I discovered the truth in Geneen Roth's books and even now, some fifty years later, I struggle with food—sometimes able to make a choice to remain present—other times succumbing to the unconscious need to cover my pain.

About six months after the molestation, my parents received notice that local authorities had dropped the charges against the painter. After sending his fingerprints to Washington, they discovered he was wanted for murder in Oklahoma and rape and sexual abuse in Long Island. At some point he was extradited to Oklahoma to face murder charges. I never did learn what happened to him.

I overheard grownups say I was lucky. Not raped, not penetrated. *No, I was just abused by a strange adult male who whispered soft things in my ear as he rubbed my vagina.* At age four, I had discovered my own vagina and how good it felt to rub it. But being touched that way at seven by an adult male changed who I was—and probably who I could have become, had I not been molested.

I suppose my parents believed if we didn't talk about the molestation, I would forget it happened. Instead, I sleep walked and talked in my sleep. A recurring nightmare in which I was being chased by a tidal wave began. I no longer enjoyed playing outside by myself. Just as I did with my parents' problems, I blamed myself for being abused. Everyone always told me how pretty I was, so I must have done something to make the painter do that to me. And although I didn't know what to call it back then, I felt ashamed because something that was obviously so wrong had felt good. Later on, therapists helped me understand that I was only seven when this occurred, too young to understand right from wrong, that the painter had broken the law, and that I was an innocent child. The most difficult aspect of the whole experience was trying to understand why pleasing sexual sensations were so wrong.

Over the years, I've thought a lot about what the painter did, how I felt at the time, and how those sensations and the way I processed them affected my sexuality. Our five senses add texture, enriching our lives. Somehow, being molested so young affected my ability to experience these senses in normal ways, thereby altering how I experienced life

18

through them. We may be drawn to the smell of freshly-made popcorn or the aroma of chocolate chip cookies baking in the oven. The taste of these things makes us feel good. Red balloons floating in the sky may cause a fluttering in our heart, and we feel like skipping along, perhaps trying to catch them. The visual experience leads to some kind of bodily reaction. Our skin responds when we cuddle a soft, fluffy teddy bear. But I have few memories of these kinds of sensations after I encountered the painter. Sexualized way too young, I pushed my sense responses deep inside, creating a chasm between sense awareness, stimulation and appropriate response.

As time went on, I understood how being sexually abused impacted my life, especially how I felt about my appearance. I began to hate how I looked. The first time I became consciously aware of how I felt was shortly after the molestation. Each summer, I spent several weeks at my cousins' house in Bridgeport, Connecticut. One hot July day, while digging sand castles at the beach, I saw a young girl (she could have been anywhere from sixteen to twenty-five) walking along the water's edge. She had long, flowing dark hair and a lovely figure. Her crying captured my attention. Following at a distance, I wondered what could make so beautiful a creature so sad. It is the first time I remember seeing another girl and wishing I looked like her. That feeling continues to haunt me, although now, at least, when I become aware of the envy, I am able to let it go.

Other effects linger. Wearing make-up still makes me uncomfortable as does primping to enhance my appearance. Questions upset me. Once someone goes beyond asking my name, I feel intruded upon and become uneasy, afraid that somehow I'll get caught in a lie or I'll be betrayed or someone will get in trouble. Being indoors is more comfortable for me than outside—I feel safer. Allowing myself sexual pleasure is often difficult. But perhaps the most troubling effect molestation had on me was my not learning to speak up for myself—especially when it came to personal boundaries. These things are somewhat easier for me now, but for many, many years, saying "No" was hard. Questioning someone when I needed clarification was scary. It was almost impossible for me to tell someone I was angry or hurt. These issues, along with my lack of self confidence, affected my ability to make appropriate choices and trust myself. How can one make the right choices when one is out of sync and out of touch with inner feelings, sensations and desires?

In *When Food is Love*, Roth talks about this situation. She says at every moment, we are choosing either to reveal ourselves or protect ourselves; to value ourselves or diminish ourselves; to tell the truth or hide. Intimacy is making the choice to be connected to, rather than isolated from, our deepest truth at that moment.

My life taught me to hide. If I revealed how I really felt, I was laughed at, mocked, or simply not understood. I became convinced that if someone discovered who I really was, they'd ridicule me like my parents had when I wanted to light Chanukah candles, or humiliate me, or leave. Between the ages of three and seven, I went from being a precocious, outgoing little girl who reveled in being the center of attention, to one who was afraid, although I had no idea what the fear was about. Therapy helped me understand that I was afraid to be pretty, afraid of my sexual feelings, afraid of rejection, and ultimately, afraid to be alone. Like a chameleon, I changed my thoughts, beliefs and feelings according to whom I was with, believing that if I acted in ways I perceived others wanted me to act, I would be loved.

What I really needed were parents who loved me unconditionally. Mine did not know how to show whatever love they felt. So I looked outside my home to find what I craved—love and attention. And if I didn't get it, I ate. As I grew older, I questioned what it was to be female, wondered how others enjoyed their sexuality, and what it must feel like to allow sexual pleasure. My joy came from eating rather than making love. As an adult, I know it is normal to become aroused and enjoy being touched by someone you love and who loves you in return, but I still struggle with allowing myself those sensations, still wanting to "hurry up and finish." The *sensations* I felt with the painter weren't wrong. I know this now. What *was* wrong was that they were brought on by an adult male touching a seven-year-old child. I can only imagine how differently my life would have played out had I received therapy after the molestation. But that's not what happened. Instead, another incident occurred, this time involving my father, which added to my little girl confusion about what it meant to be female.

Chapter 3

The Dancing Whore

<u>Queens, NY, Winter 1956</u>

I'm not sure whether my lack of memories from childhood is due
to traumatic events and the ways I learned to shut down or normal
memory loss, but the time between the molestation and adolescence is
mostly a blur. Aside from trips to court to testify, life went on as usual.
My mother went back to work when I was in second grade, so I became
a latchkey kid. I went to school, came home to an empty house, watched
television, went to bed, and listened to my parents' fight. What stands
out from that time is singing along with my 45's, making up stories for
my Ginny dolls, and dancing. After school, I would go to my downstairs
neighbor's house, and Susan and I would sing and act out roles from *South
Pacific* and *Oklahoma*. I can see now that these were creative activities
which transported me somewhere else. But back then, I was only aware
of putting on a costume and twirling around the room, which somehow
made the pain in my gut disappear for while.

* * *

"Come on, let's go," said Mom, as she shooed me out of our blue and
white 1956 Chevy Bel-Air. She held me with one hand while she juggled
the box with my ballet slippers in her other. At seven, I had already been

taking dance lessons for three years. Tonight would be my debut recital, and, bouncing up and down on the car seat, I was barely able to contain myself. On the way over, Mom explained that Dad was working, but assured me he would get to the performance on time.

We hurried backstage, and rushed to get me into my costume. I couldn't wait to get on stage. Mom handed me my ballet slippers, but my fingers shook so much, I had trouble lacing them up. She pulled out her tube of red lipstick.

"A little bit is okay," she said.

Holding up the ends of my pink tutu, I spun in front of the mirror and smiled at the image staring back at me. *I'm going to be a dancer.*

My father's booming voice echoed in the backstage halls as I heard him ask where the dancers were. As he strode towards us, I whirled around. I'd been afraid he wouldn't make it.

"You look like a whore," my father said, as he stooped to give me a hug.

I shrank inside myself, wanting to hide, to shut out the harsh words my parents threw at each other following this comment. I didn't know what the word meant, but I could tell from my mother's angry reaction that it was bad. Everything is fuzzy after that. I vaguely remember being on stage—forgetting steps and tripping over my own feet. All I could focus on was Dad's voice saying *whore.* Years later I found a photograph of me in that tutu, smiling. As I stared at the happy child in the picture, I couldn't imagine a father saying such a thing to a seven-year-old child. The only explanation which makes sense is that my dad didn't have a clue as to the impact his words had on those around him. I do know that it was the last time I liked what I saw when I looked in a mirror. That is up until Gary and I got all gussied up for a costume party. I lost thirty-eight pounds this year and bought a metallic royal blue gown with a halter top and low back. The material hugs my new figure and when I put the dress on, I felt like a 1940's movie star.

Dr. Phil McGraw says we have approximately ten defining moments in our lives that shape who we are. A defining moment, he says, is like a burn. If you lean up against a hot stove, in less than a second the event is over, but the pain can last for weeks, months. The scar can last a lifetime. The same is true for your psyche—it can be burned and disfigured. That's why if we want to understand who we are and why we do what we do, we have to go back and find those moments.

This was one of my defining moments. After my father said I looked like a whore, I went even deeper into automatic pilot mode; a part of my heart shut down. Dr. McGraw says other people come in handy—in fact, we need them. But when they stop being supportive, they can dramatically change who we are, depending on their power and relevance in our lives. Things that happen on the outside get to us on the inside, and our authentic self—which might otherwise have been doing just fine—is altered.

This incident, my being molested, and growing up with continuously battling parents fundamentally changed me. It's as if the bright-eyed, happy little dancer froze inside me—like a leaf I saw buried four feet deep in glacier ice—perfectly preserved.

I often felt a gnawing feeling in my stomach, unaware that it was anxiety or emotional pain, not hunger. Eating certain foods removed that discomfort. I learned to shut out words and conversations I didn't want to hear. Sometimes I didn't see what was right before my eyes and if I did see something unpleasant, I either blocked it out or altered the meaning in my head. Basically, my body and my mind separated.

At seven, I had not yet learned that my dad didn't necessarily mean what he said. Years later, when I did learn to speak up and ask questions, I realized it wasn't his intention to hurt me. But at the time, the way he spoke to me was like snake bites, each negative comment dripped a bit more venom into my body. After the recital, for example, he assured me that I would get ugly calf muscles from dancing—that all dancers did. A quick hug and kiss on the cheek followed that comment, a familiar pattern which followed me into adulthood: verbal abuse followed by loving affection.

During the ride home from the recital, my parents continued the argument which had begun backstage.

"You asshole," my mother said. "What the hell is the matter with you, Bill?"

"Shut up, Madeline," he said, banging his fist on the steering wheel.

"You need to watch what comes out of that mouth of yours," Mom said. "Calling your daughter a whore—what were you thinking?"

"God damn it," he screamed. "Shut the fuck up."

23

In the backseat of the car, I stroked my tutu; my hand moved back and forth, back and forth, the roughness of the netting a strong contrast with the soft satin on top of the costume. Mom turned around, asking if I was okay.

"Yes," I whispered, knowing if I said anything else it might trigger another shouting match.

For a while, we drove along in silence. I wanted this night not to have happened. I didn't ever want to dance again. The box of chocolate cupcakes in the refrigerator back home called to me and I proceeded to devour the entire thing when we got home. It's not like it was a conscious thought. It's that when I ate, the momentary pleasure of yummy tastes and a full tummy replaced the hurt inside. Using food to numb my feelings was my initiation into sleepwalking through life.

Too young to comprehend the meaning of things and unable to talk to my parents, I started right then to make poor decisions. Childhood was filled with days just like the dance recital, different scenarios but similar comments from Dad. My parents' fighting became the soundtrack of my childhood, and, at some point, I learned it wasn't entirely Dad's fault. Mom had her share in it, and as I grew older, so did I.

That was my last dance recital. I'll never know if I gave up dance due to being molested, growing up in a non-nurturing environment, being told I'd get ugly calf muscles, or some combination thereof, but I did, indeed, quit dancing. I stopped doing other things I loved, too, like drawing and making up stories. The magic of childhood ended. As I explored these issues in therapy and self-help groups, I blamed a lot of things for giving up my dreams—the man who sexually assaulted me, my father, my mother, the girl next door—anything or anyone I could find. It didn't matter who or what. Blaming others let me off the hook.

But therapy showed me that just as I was receiving negative messages from Dad about dancing, the work required to progress in dancing was increasing and I didn't want to make that commitment. Quitting was easier than putting forth that kind of effort. In addition, my parents did not show me how to think things through, to analyze situations in order to make informed decisions. They didn't know how to do that in their own lives, so how could they teach me those skills? Exploring my interests or passions was not encouraged. Decisions were made without understanding consequences. Years later, when I seriously began the therapeutic work necessary to overcome the effects of my childhood, I had to start taking responsibility for my choices and behavior. And later still, I learned to forgive the little girl who did the best she could.

In *The Four Agreements*, Don Miguel Ruiz describes the second agreement, "Don't take it personally," by telling us that if someone gives us an opinion and says, "'Hey, you look so fat,'" don't take it personally, because the truth is that this person is dealing with his or her own feelings, beliefs and opinions. That person tried to send poison to you, and, if you take it personally, then you take that poison and it becomes yours. But, according to Ruiz, if you do not take it personally, you are immune in the middle of hell.

During my childhood, I swallowed a lot of poison from others and some nasty seeds were planted in my soul—seeds that sprouted as assumptions which grew into incorrect beliefs. Today I hear friends tell their children that they can do anything they want if they work hard. I did not hear those words from my parents, or teachers for that matter. So, with no healthy adult role models, I escaped into a world of television, books, movies and music. Again, this was the 1950's. Patsy Cline sang "*I go out walking after midnight searching for you.*" Brenda Lee crooned, "*All alone am I, ever since your goodbye.*" Connie Francis wondered where the boys were, convinced "*someone waits for me.*" In movies, Marilyn Monroe and Jane Russell tried to marry millionaires and Lana Turner lived in fear in Peyton Place that her secret—that she was an unwed mother—would surface and she'd be ostracized. Song lyrics and story lines fostered in me the notion that women were dependent on men and that I'd better follow society's rules. Women were supposed to be virgins when they married, then have babies. And by all means, they were to *stand by* their *man*, as Tammy Wynette did in her popular song.

By age seven, I understood that self-expression had gotten me into trouble. Escape was far safer. I didn't experience unconditional love, so I believed the fictional love shown in movies, television, and books, and I couldn't wait to grow up. I would be a wife and mother like Jane Wyatt on "Father Knows Best" or Donna Reed on "The Donna Reed Show." In my childish fantasy, once that occurred, I'd have a husband who took care of me and children who loved and looked up to me. But in the meantime, there remained a starving little girl who hungered for love and attention. And unfortunately, she learned all the wrong ways to receive it.

Chapter 4

"You Have To Be A Virgin
When You Get Married!"

<u>Queens, NY 1961</u>

"Now then, class," said Mr. Plotkin, my seventh grade math teacher
at P.S. 218.
"You take…"
Mr. Plotkin's voice drifted towards outer space. I tried to bring it back
into the classroom, but my eyes strayed out the window. Mr. Plotkin drew
lines around numbers, crossed some numbers off while writing others
above the line. Roz and Shelley, two girls I wanted to know because they
were beautiful and smart, kept raising their hands to answer questions.
*They'll never want to be friends with me. I'm so stupid I don't understand
anything the teacher is saying. Maybe you should raise your hand and ask
him to explain it again,* said a quiet voice inside my head. *Maybe you
should just shut up,* came another. *Want her to embarrass herself in front
of all these kids? She'll never fit in that way, you jerk.*
The clamor inside my head grew louder. My heart beat faster. I started
to raise my hand, wanting to say I didn't understand, but something
pulled it back down. The numbers on the board grew fuzzy, and Mr.
Plotkin's voice came from across an ocean, drowned out by crashing
waves pounding the sand.
"Karen, what did you come up with?" Mr. Plotkin asked, strutting

down the row like a penguin, his Phi Beta Kappa key staring me in the face.

My throat tightened and I held my breath. There was nothing written on my clean white notebook with the extra wide lines. I hadn't even tried to solve the problem. I didn't know the first step. But I couldn't say that out loud. Everyone would know how stupid I was.

"I'm not finished yet, Mr. Plotkin. I need a few more minutes."

He smiled and crooked his finger at me, nodding his head towards the blackboard. As I stood robot-like in front of my classmates for what felt like hours, the heat of a blush spread up my neck and across my face. I was unable to solve the algebraic equation.

Bruce, the tallest and shyest boy in our class, came to my aid, moving up to the front of the classroom while the teacher gestured for me to go back to my seat. A few short minutes later, after Bruce had correctly completed the equation on the board, Mr. Plotkin thanked him. My heart slowed back down to normal, my breathing evened out, my eyes could once again see the numbers on the blackboard clearly, and the roar in my head subsided. When Bruce explained how he arrived at the answer, I got it. I could see how it worked. But when Mr. Plotkin put the next problem up, I didn't have a clue how to solve it.

Brnggggg. Recess! Thank God. Grabbing my books, I ran outside. Roz and Shelley sat at a table, quietly talking and eating their lunches. On a nearby bench, Bruce poured over his math book. Other kids sat in cliques around the yard. Alone again, I slid my books under the bench behind the swings and climbed up. My foot slipped on a bright yellow leaf as I pushed off. Pumping hard, I soared, the crisp fall air whipping over my face. The tops of the trees were bare. It wouldn't be long before all the leaves were gone and winter would come. I welcomed winter. I could stay indoors, where nothing could hurt me.

* * *

As I headed back inside for my next class, Betty, my close friend since we were eight, joined me. We had English together next period.

"Want to come over after school today?" Betty asked. She lived across the street from me. It had been her mother who'd told me about Chanukah.

27

"Sure," I replied. *Maybe Betty's mom would ask how school was today. No one was home at my house—and even if they were, they wouldn't ask.*

I wished Betty's older brother, Steve, could explain math to me. But I did not ask for help that day or any other day. Instead, I continued to "zone out" when I missed something, afraid to speak up, afraid of what others would think. This phenomenon seeped into other areas of my life as I got older, particularly relationships. When I shut down, I avoided the pain of not being listened to, not being heard. I did not hear my father's insults or the ridicule from the many boys/men who came and went in my life. I know now this kind of repression isn't healthy. It's like each negative comment became a piece of fat on my body, an accumulation of anger and hurt I never expressed. The fat eventually became a way for me to hide. Going to that numb state became an unhealthy tool I used to avoid confrontation.

Eventually I understood that my inability to speak up was ultimately a fear of being left alone. If I kept the peace, relationships remained intact—dysfunctional, but intact. Not understanding algebra was only the beginning of a long line of situations in which I chose to remain silent rather than risk self-exposure or being left. Thankfully, I am now learning to reveal myself when I'm confused, disagreed with, or want to make a statement about something. Algebra, however, remains a mystery.

* * *

As I grew into adolescence, I had no idea being sexually abused had affected my feelings, my behavior, and the decisions I subsequently made. Boys began to look at me a certain way shortly after my first menstrual period. Several years earlier, my mother had given me the book, *Growing up and Liking It*. But at eleven, when I woke up one morning with blood all over my sheets, my mother came into my room and slapped me across the face. The book hadn't explained *that* part of becoming a woman.

It turns out this was some sort of tradition in Judaism, supposedly meant to welcome a young girl into womanhood. Unfortunately, I didn't feel welcomed at all. I had severe cramps and wanted hugs and loving attention, not a slap in the face. The strange thing is that my mother was agnostic and didn't believe in God, so for her to have done something relating to Judaism seems bizarre to me now. At the time, the slap simply stung, literally and figuratively. She didn't explain why she did it and I didn't ask.

When I related this incident to my first editor, Dina, she said, "I'm Jewish and I've never heard of such a thing." We thought maybe my mother, given her rather odd child-rearing ideas, had made it up. But when we researched in Google, we found articles relating to this. One, by Caren Apple-Slingbaum, says slapping is an old Jewish custom—a *minhag* in Hebrew. Slingbaum questioned if its original purpose was to 'slap sense' into a newly fertile girl, warning her not to disgrace the family by becoming pregnant out of wedlock. Perhaps it was to "awaken" her out of her childhood slumber and into her role as a Jewish woman.

Slingbaum also stated that while many rabbis assured her that this slapping custom was not in accordance with Jewish law, it was a tradition that had been well guarded and nurtured for generations. Yet Slingbaum questioned the efficacy of this ritual, saying, "…even so, a slap—as in any brutal act—brings about shame and humiliation." Slingbaum went on to ask why we should have to equate those emotions with our bodies and our lifeblood.

Why indeed? As I moved through my teen years, shame and humiliation moved with me, gradually taking up more and more space inside. There were many reasons. Adolescents grapple with a myriad of emotions while hormones race through their bodies. I was uncomfortable inside my own skin. In an attempt to change that (mistakenly thinking if I liked how I looked, I'd be happy), I put soda cans in my hair trying to remove the curls. I also ironed it. I tried make-up, but in the back of my mind I heard Dad saying, *whore*, so that didn't work. At the beach, I'd arrange my body in such a way that my weight distributed to not show flab. The ironic thing was that I wasn't heavy yet. I didn't start gaining weight until I got married at nineteen. Dad always had a comment though, no matter what I did. It felt like he did not want me to be pretty.

"You're so skinny, if you turn sideways you'll disappear," he said at one point.

Some part of me still believes I'm better off bulky so I won't disappear. As a young girl around my father, if I gained weight, I was too fat. If I lost weight, I was too skinny. If I cut my hair, it was too short. If I let it grow, I should cut it. At the same time, I was Jewish, with curly dark hair and freckles while the Beach Boys sang about blonde surfer girls and Yvette Mimeaux was the ideal. My father's comments, along with the cultural images displayed in movies and magazines, deeply affected how I felt about being female and fostered an inability to feel good about myself, no matter how many people said I was attractive.

Perhaps my father was terrified because I had been sexually assaulted and didn't know how to deal with that appropriately. Or maybe, as some therapists might suggest, he was sexually attracted to me. I'll never know. What I do know is that I grew up hating my body, shutting down healthy sexual feelings, and creating relationships in which I did not feel loved or respected.

I wanted attention from boys, but when I received it, my stomach hurt or my heart raced. As early as eleven or twelve years old, I obsessed and felt bad about not having boyfriends. Because of the molestation, I was aware of my sexuality at an earlier than normal age and sadly, negative experiences with boys started right away. Crushes were not reciprocated; the object of my attention usually liked the cute girls I envied.

Rejection came for the first time in Junior High. Our school had a ninth grade prom and none of the popular boys invited me. At the last minute, an overweight boy named Dan asked me to go with him. Because I desperately wanted to go to the prom, I accepted. Looking back, I can see that I was drawn to the cute, bad boys and couldn't care less about the down-home nice ones—those who were raised to treat girls nicely. Dan wasn't handsome, but he was a gentleman. I went to the prom with him feeling ugly, inadequate, rejected and definitely unpopular.

* * *

As a teen, one of my favorite movies was *Splendor in the Grass,* with Natalie Wood and Warren Beatty. It came out in 1963, when I was fourteen. They portrayed teenagers in 1928 that were deeply in love, but the morals of the times prevented the Natalie Wood character from "going all the way." When they break up, she has a nervous breakdown. The movie brought out the issue of "good girls" versus "bad girls"—illustrating the belief that if a girl had sexual feelings and acted on them, she was bad. In the movie, Natalie Wood's mother tells her that sex is something only men enjoy and women endure. My mother had given me the same message. It was wrong unless I was married, and if I married, I should just put up with it—that women do not necessarily like or enjoy sex. At some point in my early teens, I remember my father telling me my mother was frigid. One therapist told me that an inappropriate sexual comment like that from a parent was a form of emotional incest. At the time, I didn't know these kinds of comments were abnormal; that my parents' were flawed; that their parenting skills left a lot to be desired, and that my thoughts and feelings about myself were flawed as a result of all these things. I simply thought I was flawed.

As bad as life was in junior high, though, high school was even worse. I attended Forest Hills High, one of the top ten public high schools in the country at that time. For some strange reason, it had sororities and fraternities, and mostly rich, snooty kids went there. I wasn't one of them—my family was definitely lower middle class. My friends and I tried out for one particular sorority. It involved going to the house of one of the rich girls, being placed in the center of the room, and subjecting ourselves to an interrogation. I don't remember the questions or the experience because I numbed out. I sensed I wasn't responding the way the sorority girls wanted, but I answered the questions truthfully. As I write this, I think what probably happened was that I flashed back to the painter and being interrogated by police detectives. Being questioned somehow triggers a feeling that I've done something wrong. And being the center or focus of attention triggers acute anxiety—my heart pounds, my breath becomes shallow, and if I try to speak, my voice cracks. Even today, my self-esteem sometimes slips away when I am the object of someone's attention or responding to questions. Back then, it disappeared completely.

My friends were accepted into the sorority while I was not. In that moment, another part of my heart closed down. With no one to tell me differently, I assumed there was something deeply wrong with me. I'd answered honestly and I was rejected. On the outside I looked normal enough, but inside, my heart and brain worked differently than others. I didn't get jokes, my feelings got hurt when someone else might just laugh a comment off. I liked books and movies others hated and didn't like those others loved. I was the ugly duckling who would never become the swan—all of which fanned the fires of self-hatred burning in my soul.

* * *

31

Around this time, my mother began preaching about being a virgin when I got married. She emphasized how important it was, so I decided to listen. Despite being a latchkey kid and therefore frequently alone, my mother did still exert control over me. I remember asking her whether I liked certain foods or not—if she said no, I wouldn't eat it and vice versa. In my later teens, she inspected my sheets for signs of sexual activity. And I could be controlled by her moods and facial expressions.

But hungry for attention, especially from boys, I rebelled in my own way, becoming the kind of girl who was willing to do anything and everything a boy wanted, except have intercourse. Aside from my prom date with Dan, no one asked me out, and I desperately wanted a boyfriend. At fifteen, I had a huge crush on Betty's seventeen-year-old brother, Steve. One day I went to Betty's house after school. She wasn't home, but Steve was in his room in the basement of their two-story house.

"Who's there?" he called.

"Karen," I answered, "from across the street."

He invited me down. Steve was sprawled on his bed, books and notebooks scattered everywhere. He patted the bed, indicating I should sit down.

"Come on, don't worry, I won't bite," he said. I sat, trembling inside. It was the first time a boy I liked showed interest in me. I know we must have talked about something, but I don't remember what. The next thing I recall is Steve kissing me. His tongue burrowed deep in my mouth, his hands roamed all over my body. Opening his zipper, he placed my hand on his penis, huge and throbbing. Pushing my head down, he explained what he wanted me to do next. When he finished, he gave me a quick hug and said Betty would be home later.

Over the next few weeks, I continued to see Steve down in his basement room, hiding the truth from Betty. Steve insisted we keep it private. I'm not sure why it ended, but I know Steve never took me out on a date, never told me I was pretty, and hardly ever spoke to me after our interludes ended. But he must have talked to someone, because a short time later, his friend, Mike, asked me out, and Mike expected the same sexual behavior Steve had. Desperate to be wanted and liked, I complied. The best way I can explain this behavior is that I had no voice. Speaking up had gotten me tortured as a child. Questioning what was expected of me had only gotten me in trouble. My auto-pilot circuitry was programmed to do what others wanted and needed to make them happy. I learned to ignore my needs, and eventually lost awareness of them altogether. And "No" was simply not in my vocabulary.

My sexual initiation was begun by an adult male when I was seven years old. Steve and Mike were the next males to pay attention to me sexually. But they weren't the only boys I humiliated myself with, hoping to attract a boyfriend. There were many others. My goal was to gain their acceptance and attention, but the more I gave in to their requests, the worse I felt about myself—dirty and ashamed, but unable to stop. No connection was made between my sexual behavior with boys and the growing negative feelings I had about myself. I had no knowledge of sexual intimacy and what that can and should be like.

I wish my mother had spoken with me about sex and sexuality. Other than the basic "where do babies come from" talk that occurred around age eight, and insisting I be a virgin when I got married, she didn't discuss female sexuality. To be fair, I don't believe my mother's female relatives talked to her about sex either. Mom's mother had died when Mom was ten and in those days people didn't talk about sex at all. So anything I discovered about sexuality, I learned on my own. And given my upbringing and the culture of the time, my perceptions, beliefs and attitudes were skewed and misguided.

* * *

Chapter 5

First Soul Connection

Queens, New York 1965

I stared at the silky brown hair cascading down her back and wished it were mine. Mr. Justin was reading "O Captain, My Captain" to our eleventh grade English class at Forest Hills High School. I was 16, and Carol had come into class that day with an attitude.

"Look at that," I whispered to Betty. "Her ankle bracelet looks just like mine."

Carol turned around, her almond eyes glaring at me. Smiling, I shifted my gaze downward. Periodically, during the rest of the class, Carol turned to look at me, and when class was over, she followed me out.

"I noticed you watching me today," she said. "I wondered why."

Why? How could I tell her I wished my black, curly hair was more like hers; that her bubbly personality made me feel shyer than I already was? Instead, I said, "I was just admiring your ankle bracelet." Lifting my leg, I showed her the gold and pearl bracelet adorning my left ankle.

Carol smiled a smile that lit up the hallway. "Can I have your phone number? We can talk tonight," she said.

Scribbling my number on a piece of paper, I shoved it at her, never expecting her to call. But that night she did. I don't remember that first conversation, but I do recall giggling over everything and nothing.

"We're having a giggle fit," Carol said, when we had stopped laughing long enough to speak.

Every night, after dinner and homework, I closed the door to my room, got into bed, and either called Carol or waited for her to call. My pink Princess phone glowed softly in the dark as we talked and laughed late into the night.

Our friendship blossomed through that year and into the next. If we weren't spending time just the two of us, we double-dated with our boyfriends. I was seeing Louis (the boy from the orthodox family I mentioned in the introduction). There's not a lot to say about him except that Louis was my first real boyfriend. Steve and Mike had never taken me out and our "relationship" was purely about sex—and more specifically, about my providing sexual pleasure for them. My relationship with Louis, which lasted two years, helped shape the form my relationships would take from then on, until I woke up sufficiently to change my behavior. What I mean is, my choices were always those who didn't share the same level of feeling I had, or it was someone incapable of showing love at all, or someone who lied about their feelings or behavior.

One day, shortly after senior year began, Carol noticed a lump in her neck. "My doctor says it's nothing," Carol said. "But I don't know."

Six months later, when it still hadn't gone away, her mother, Margaret, consulted another doctor.

"I need a biopsy," Carol told me. At seventeen, I didn't understand what that meant.

The day before Carol was to have the test, we went to the park with her mother. The sky was blue, and many of the leaves had already fallen from the trees. As it was cold for October, the park was deserted. Carol and I didn't say much; we simply enjoyed being with each other, playing hopscotch and potsy, eating double-scooped ice cream cones, and holding hands while skipping around the park scrunching leaves and completing each other's sentences.

Margaret was an attractive widow, and a lot of things my mother wasn't. Mom had grown frumpy, her hair now a mousy brown. She had a dumpy figure and rarely applied make-up any more. In contrast, Margaret had jet black hair streaked with silver, wore tailored clothing, never left the house without make-up, and got dressed just to take the garbage out. We became friends, too. She would talk to me about the horrible things that had happened to her, starting with her husband's early death at age thirty-five. But mostly, she talked about her son, Larry, who was four years older than Carol and I. Early on in my friendship with Carol I'd met Larry, but since he was engaged to someone else, he made no impression. Besides, I had Louis, who took me to nice restaurants, bought me pretty jewelry, and cheated on me regularly.

A few days after Carol's biopsy, I called to find out the results.

"Carol's very sick," Margaret said. "She has Hodgkin's Disease."

"What does that mean?" I asked.

"It's cancer of the lymph glands and you can die from it," she said, mentioning a famous baseball player who had died from Hodgkin's.

Carol and I called each other "halfie" because we frequently knew what the other was thinking. Until I'd met her, I'd been on the outside of life looking in, my nose pressed up against the glass, wanting what those on the other side had. With Carol, I felt connected, and what I was hearing was that she could die. My screams brought my mother running into my room, but I was inconsolable. She grabbed the phone and spoke with Margaret awhile. I don't know what she said; I was sobbing hysterically. The next thing I remember is my mother handing me the phone saying Carol's brother, Larry, wanted to speak to me. I've forgotten his words, but they calmed me down. It was the first time I felt nurtured by an adult male.

After the biopsy, Carol needed frequent chemotherapy and radiation treatments at Mt. Sinai Hospital. Since both her mother and brother worked, I drove Carol from where we lived in Queens to her treatments in Manhattan, practically moving in with them so I could help. The radiation made Carol very sick. At home, I stood by her in the shower as she threw up, watching the clumps of her beautiful brown hair fall onto the white tile floor. I can still see the lines of blue ink on her chest, mapping the area from her earlobes to below her stomach that were to receive radiation.

"I don't know what we'd do without you," Carol said one day, her arms wrapped around me. That night I slept over and the framed poster of bare-chested Paul Newman in *Hud* smiled down from between the twin beds. We used to tease one another over who loved him more. It was one of many connections, as well as our mutual love of *West Side Story*. We'd each seen it nine times before we'd ever met and would end up seeing it three more times together.

36

My friendship with Carol provided comfort and joy in ways I'd never known. I was welcomed, not just by Carol, but by her whole family. Our friendship, and the way I participated in Carol's care, opened parts of me which had been shut down since I was seven.

But Carol's family chose not to tell her how serious the illness was, and I had to pretend as well. My mother said she could never forgive Margaret for how she had told me about Carol's illness, and for forcing me to lie to my best friend. But what I focused on was the fact that Margaret could talk to me because I cared about her daughter almost as much as she did and that I felt like I made a difference to both of them. Still, it *was* an awkward position in which to place a seventeen-year-old girl. My mother was probably right, but I also believe my mother was jealous. And frankly, I don't blame her for that; she had every right to be.

I became somewhat obsessed with Carol and her family. At her house nearly every day, I got to know her grandparents and her brother, Larry, a bit, too. Poppy (Carol's grandfather) fell in love with me and decided he wanted me for a granddaughter. By this time I'd broken up with my boyfriend Louis.

I began to notice Larry, who was tall and thin, with thick, black, wavy hair. He had brown eyes, a prominent nose, and sported the long sideburns which were popular then—like John Lennon's.

Larry's family disliked the girl to whom he was engaged, so Poppy campaigned to somehow bring Larry and me together. One night my car wouldn't start. Poppy lent Larry his car but told him he could only take me home; he couldn't go to his fiancée's house afterward. It was a Friday night and she was expecting Larry, but he never arrived.

Instead, Larry drove me to King's Point in Great Neck, where we connected for three hours. We talked, mostly about how unhappy he was. But he didn't want to break his engagement because then she would keep the ring he'd given her. Larry said if she broke it off, by law, she would have to return it.

This should have been my first warning signal, but I ignored it. There were other red flags as well. Once, for example, I saw Larry throw Carol across a room. Another time he cursed and belittled his mother in front of me. Now, with hindsight and the wisdom of age, I understand why I ignored those signals. If I had allowed myself to register what these signs meant, I would probably not have married Larry, and that's what I wanted most. It felt like I had no choice. Marriage was my way out of my parents' miserable home. It would fulfill my childhood fantasy—when I married, I'd finally be loved. And I did feel loved by Carol's family.

After King's Point, Larry drove back to his apartment, where he still lived with Margaret and Carol. He was twenty-two and worked as an accountant for a large oil company. Except for one semester at college, he had always lived at home. We walked in holding hands. Margaret, Carol, and Grammy and Poppy waited for us, pleased to see we apparently were taking Poppy's wishes to heart. We saw each other every night for the next week. I frequently sat on Larry's lap; there was lots of hugging and kissing. And he was still engaged.

The following week, Larry visited his fiancée while I waited at his apartment. Carol was back in the hospital for some additional treatments, so Margaret and I sat together. I remember being more excited than nervous, though I don't recall details. I know Larry was gone for several hours and when he got home, he said, "Well, I'm free now, maybe I'll call Stephanie" (an old girlfriend). It should have been obvious that Larry wasn't interested in a relationship with me, but at the time, I didn't want to acknowledge it. I wanted to become part of a family that loved me and Larry was my ticket in.

But he didn't call Stephanie. After his engagement ended, Larry dated no one but me, so I interpreted his exclusiveness as true love. We immediately started "going steady" and his family was ecstatic. Mine was not. My mother was jealous of my closeness to Carol and Margaret, and my father thought Larry a sissy because he went into the National Guard to avoid being drafted. This was 1967, the height of the Vietnam War. On the nightly news, we were bombarded with images of boys carrying guns, slogging through jungles, shooting Vietnamese soldiers as well as civilian men, women and children. We knew boys who had enlisted, boys threatening to go to Canada, and others who, like Larry, did what they could to avoid active combat duty.

Every night of Larry's basic training, he called to complain about his experience, wanting to come home. My father, a veteran of World War II, understandably had a hard time with this behavior. Years later I would realize that Dad was right about Larry, but at the time I was eighteen and had already made up my mind that my parents' didn't know what they were talking about most of the time. Besides, I thought I had fallen

38

in love. So I pressed on. When I told Larry that I loved him, he refused to say he loved me, unwilling to make that commitment.

The following year, we were invited to the wedding of a friend of Larry's. The event was to take place in October. I was in my second year at Queensborough Community College, working towards an Associate degree in Applied Science when a friend invited me on a trip to Nassau, Bahamas during fall break. Since my family had only vacationed in the Catskills, the Caribbean would be a new experience. Besides, it wouldn't hurt for Larry to miss me a little during the ten days I'd be gone.

On the morning of the wedding, Larry arrived to drive me to the beauty parlor. As I climbed into the car, Larry looked at me and said, "Do you want to get married?" Stunned, I sat in disbelief for the next few minutes while Larry tried to convince me he was serious. At the curb in front of the beauty shop, I got out of the car. As Larry drove off, I ran after the car, yelling "But you never even said 'I love you!'"

Years later, when I began to examine my feelings and actions during that time, I could admit I had manipulated Larry. Knowing he was terrified of being alone—the way he'd handled his basic training had shown me that—I surmised that if I went away, he'd commit to me. I was right, but the price I paid was a desperately unhappy marriage and a downhill slide into depression.

The truth is I don't think Larry ever loved me. Nor do I think I loved him. It's easy now to comprehend what happened, but I was oblivious then to my feelings, as well as those of others. Being a bride, having a nice wedding, fixing up an apartment and keeping house was all I'd ever wanted, so I couldn't let myself even think about the possibility of not marrying Larry. His behavior towards the women in his life should have propelled me to keep my distance. But I told myself he would change, convinced he would be loving and kind with me. It is a prime example of what John Lennon wrote about in his song, *"Living is easy with eyes closed, misunderstanding all you see."* If I had told myself the truth buried inside me, I wouldn't have gotten what I thought I wanted and needed.

The friendship with Carol reveals a lot about me at the time. I loved her so much that I gave up thoughts of myself to help her and her family. I loved Margaret, too, who was in so much pain that I would do anything to ease it. Larry was miserable too, as were my parents, whom I had unsuccessfully tried to make happy. By marrying Larry, I simply did what I had always done—tried to fix other peoples' problems instead of focusing on me. But I wouldn't learn about this type of behavior until after I lost custody of my child some nine years later. In the recovery field, it is called "rescuing" and in my experience, it doesn't work. Some people call it "people pleasing"—usually done to obtain someone else's love and approval. This doesn't work either. Unless people ask for help, jumping in and trying to fix them usually causes resentment and ultimately withdrawal by the friends you are trying to help. But at the time, I believed if I was good to all those around me, they would love me unconditionally. And moreover, the love would last forever. My inability to feel and relate in normal healthy ways would rear its ugly head in major ways once Larry and I got married, because like my parents before me, when two people with dysfunctional backgrounds come together, it is a recipe for failure.

Chapter 6

A Match *Not* Made in Heaven

New York 1969

On my wedding day, back in 1969, I awoke and bolted upright in bed. A voice inside my head screamed, *Oh my God, what are you doing?* It was a voice I'd heard before when doubts niggled at me. *You are making a mistake*, it said. But images of the Larry I thought I'd fallen in love with—the man who pulled me onto his lap to comfort me when Carol's Hodgkin's disease caused her hair to fall out, who wrapped his grandfather in his arms and kissed the top of his bald head—came to mind. Another voice whispered *He loves you.* So which voice was I supposed to listen to? One hundred and fifty guests were expected and my parents had spent a fortune on the wedding; I couldn't back out. The whisper of wisdom penetrated the protective numbness I'd created, but I refused to follow its advice. Instead, I gave in to the voice of the needy child saying, *This is what you've always wanted. Now you will be happy.* On the morning of my wedding a veil hung over me, distorting my vision. Instead of honoring what I knew and calling it off, I slipped into denial along with my wedding dress.

* * *

The wedding took place on a Sunday afternoon, and the ceremony and reception were over by five o'clock that evening. Since we hadn't

41

eaten much at the reception, we went to a diner with Carol and her fiancé, returning home around eight to watch *War of the Worlds*. Needless to say, this wasn't very romantic. We had made no honeymoon plans. Everyone thought we were going away, but instead, we stayed in our new apartment getting acquainted as husband and wife.

Later that night, when Larry couldn't penetrate me, a loud voice in my head said, *You're such a freak. You're not normal.*

Uneducated about sexuality, I didn't know that during foreplay, women are supposed to become aroused and lubricate. That didn't happen for me, so intercourse was painful that first time and remained so for over a year. I hated making love until we discovered Vaseline, which helped somewhat; it made it painless, but not pleasurable. I remained unresponsive our entire marriage. In those days, it wasn't common for women to talk to each other about sex, so I had no idea what was normal. It became one more way I felt different from other women. Unaware that my having been sexually abused as a child had affected my ability to have healthy adult sexual relationships, Larry and I both suffered. I hadn't told him (or anyone else), about the molestation.

Our marriage was empty, just like the sex. We had no emotional intimacy and really didn't communicate much. Larry talked—I listened. I didn't know how to express myself or share feelings in a healthy manner, so I kept quiet, building resentments and withdrawing more and more.

Early on, Larry insulted me. The first time he saw me naked in the light, he said I had "ugly boobs with big fat hairy nipples." I also had a fat nose, short teeth, sharp elbows, flabby arms, a big stomach and ass, and hairy legs. Over time, he called me stupid, klutzy, and fat. At 5' 3 ½" and one hundred nineteen pounds I was anything but fat, but believed every nasty word he said about me.

Convinced I was a horrible monster who was lucky Larry married me (*who else would have me*), I gained weight, dressed frumpily, never wore makeup, and kept the negative feelings to myself. Depression burned into my soul like slow-moving lava down a mountain side. What saved me were the monthly gatherings with three other couples. One Sunday a month, we'd meet at one of our houses to play canasta. After the card game, we shared a meal. My favorite part of the day, though, was when the eight of us switched from urban young married couples to become "The Dippos." We'd put on our favorite records and sing along. At least that's the way it started. Invariably, while we girls sang seriously, the guys would cut up, each one acting sillier than the next, creating hysterics in them. In the tapes we made of these sessions, you can hear their efforts to get us to stop singing, to no avail. In a recent conversation with Larry, he asked me if I could still reach the high note in *"Here, There, and Everywhere,"* my favorite Beatle song. And I can still see him standing on the deck of the Staten Island Ferry with his friend, Bob, singing *"I Should Have Known Better with a Girl like You,"* imitating John Lennon quite effectively. It was one of the moments that made me think I was in love with him.

* * *

July 1969

Until I got married and learned how to cook, my kitchen forays were limited to wolfing down six Yankee Doodle cupcakes for breakfast while making tuna fish sandwiches to take to school for lunch. Neither of my parents knew how to cook, so dinners were bland meals: broiled hamburgers with no spices and spaghetti with sauce from a jar, or hotdogs—meals my father prepared that didn't require much effort. My mother knew how to make one thing, meatloaf, but we didn't have it often. Mostly we ate out, alternating between Chinese and Italian restaurants. I don't remember a single time we had company for dinner. I thought it was the white appliances, white cabinets, and white Formica counter-tops that made our kitchen a cold, stark place. But it was the absence of love; our kitchen had no heart.

I was learning to cook from my mother-in-law, Margaret. Larry and I had been married three months and so far I'd mastered Italian meatballs and spaghetti.

"I'm bringing a colleague home for dinner," Larry said one morning as we got ready for work.

"I was planning to try your mother's beef stew tonight, but I've never made it before. Is that all right?"

This would be my first time cooking for company. Larry assured me it would be fine and we left for work, walking together to the subway station in downtown Flushing, where we rode the #7 train into Woodside.

There we parted ways. Larry took the IRT subway downtown to the Wall Street area, where he was an accountant while I rode the F train to midtown Manhattan, where I was a secretary.

That evening I left work early to prepare for the dinner party. I gathered the ingredients—beef cubes, onions, garlic, canned tomatoes, potatoes, carrots, and ketchup—and tossed them in the pressure cooker, adding some water before closing the lid and putting the little top on the piece that stuck up from the lid. Crossing my fingers, I turned the heat on the stove, hoping it came out as good as Margaret's. Larry arrived home a few minutes later and introduced me to the co-worker and his wife. While I remained in the kitchen putting a salad together, they sat in the living room chatting. About twenty minutes later, the buzzer went off, signaling the beef stew was ready.

The aroma of beef, tomatoes, and garlic filled the kitchen and everyone commented on how good it smelled. This was one way my marriage would be different than my parents'. My house would be filled with friends and family—a house of joy rather than a battle field. I twisted the lid on the pressure cooker and started to lift the cover when the little top piece flew off, steam exploded out of the pot, and the beef stew splattered across the walls, the ceiling, the counters, the floor, and the cabinets of my lovely kitchen. No one had told me you had to remove the little top to relieve pressure prior to removing the lid.

Sinking to the floor, my tears mingled with pieces of tomatoes, onion, and beef, and once more I was the latchkey kid who only knew how to make tuna fish. It wasn't the first or the last time I slipped into childhood mode due to stress or trauma. In reality, I had just turned twenty and was living in my first apartment with its turquoise appliances and bleached oak cabinets. I'd fallen in love with the place because of the kitchen. I have no memory after sinking to the floor, crying. Nor do I remember cleaning up the beef stew splatter, or what we did about dinner that night. Larry's reaction and how he treated me during and after the kitchen disaster elude me as well. Conversations are blurred. I don't even remember what the couple looked like, or what they said when the beef stew exploded. I know we never saw them again. Freud says we censor memories that are too traumatic and I believe him.

The things I do remember about how Larry treated me during our marriage are not pleasant, so I can't imagine he reacted well to my failure in front of a colleague. Humiliated and ashamed, I remember thinking perhaps my parents had it right: eating out was a good idea. I didn't know until my mother died in 2001 that she even owned a table cloth. I inherited that, along with two sets of silverware which we had never used while I was growing up. Gary and I use them a lot now, though, as we entertain quite frequently.

It was a long time before I attempted to cook for company again. The marriage, wrong from the start, did not improve with time. I continued to experiment with recipes, some from my mother-in-law, some from cookbooks, some from friends. Eventually, I became a fair cook, but never learned to love cooking. Searching for a family I never had, I wanted a kitchen where people who loved each other gathered together—where eating was secondary to sharing and laughing and telling stories about each other's day.

Marriage had been a way to escape the barrage of fighting between my parents and the tension that lived and breathed in every room of their house. Wanting a loving home, I believed that, if I loved Larry enough, I'd get what I wanted. But neither Larry nor I knew what love was. Until that point, Carol was the only one who seemed to love me unconditionally. Never having had loving relationships, I tried to create one by making my kitchen a warm, inviting place, thinking that was what was needed. Thousands of meals were cooked in three different kitchens during my marriage to Larry, which lasted almost nine years. But a loving home remained elusive.

* * *

1972

Our marriage had its ups and downs, but when Larry got fired from his position at the oil company, things took a turn for the worse. He never explained the reason for his dismissal. Instead, he moped around, not doing much to find a new job and made himself and others, especially me, miserable. At the time the following event occurred, it had been nine months since Larry lost his job. We had been married about three years.

Our apartment was silent unless you counted the sound of traffic on Parsons Blvd, which never stopped. New York is the city that never sleeps, after all, and Flushing, Queens is part of New York. Propped up on my pillows, I leaned upright against the headboard. It was the fourth night in a row I was awake at 2:00 am, waiting for Larry to come home. I tried to sleep, but when I closed my eyes, white lights flashed in the darkness and a roar in my ears like distant thunder caused my feet and hands to twitch, making me restless.

"You're still up," Larry said, as he slowly walked into our bedroom. He sat on the edge of the bed and removed his shoes and socks.

"Where were you?"

Continuing his methodical movements, Larry removed one piece of clothing, then the next, never once looking at me. If his shoulders slumped any more, they'd touch the floor. Tension oozed from his body.

"I was at Shelley's," he said. Shelley and Victor were both friends of mine since junior high school and I knew Victor was away on National Guard Duty. They were one of the four couples from our monthly canasta gathering. Larry finished undressing, climbed into bed and turned on his side, his back to me.

"Larry, what's going on? It's the middle of the night. For three weeks you've been coming home at all hours. Talk to me. Please."

He took a slow, deep breath and rolled over, the lamplight making shadows across his face. His eyes looked past mine, fixed somewhere behind me.

"Karen, I don't know if I love you any more. I don't know if I ever did. I think I'm in love with Shelley."

"I'm outta here, you fucking bastard," I said, surprising both of us. Throwing the covers off, I scrambled out of bed and began jamming clothes into a suitcase. Since my parents were on vacation, I had the key to their apartment. Larry's eyes opened wide and he popped up. He didn't try to stop me and I was grateful he was not screaming obscenities or insults, his typical mode of communication. I was also glad I did not shout back or lie there mute. Fifteen minutes later, I struggled with the door to my parents' apartment, my hand shaking so hard I could not get the key in the keyhole. Throwing my suitcase on the sofa, I barely made it to the bathroom before throwing up.

Leaning against the bathtub, I waited for my stomach pains to subside. Caked-on dirt around the bottom of the toilet bowl; black ring marks around the tub; dust bunnies under the sink—I made a mental note to talk to Mom about getting a housecleaner. The next few hours were spent scrubbing my parents' bathroom from top to bottom. The kitchen was tackled next. Sunlight streamed in through the living room window as I hauled the vacuum cleaner out of the front closet. I watched the mouth of the vacuum cleaner suck up clumps of dust and dirt, wishing my life could be cleaned up so easily. Bitterly disappointed that marriage had not brought me the love I'd expected, I did not know what to do.

Unable to distinguish between messages from Spirit and parental, peer or societal pressure, I wavered between wanting this marriage to work and knowing that it couldn't. Four days later, my mother-in-law convinced me to give Larry another chance. Listening to her instead of Spirit, I postponed the inevitable. To be fair to myself at that time, however, I had not pursued the spiritual peace I'd found lighting Chanukah candles in childhood. Larry was not religious; nor had my family been. I had no idea how to connect to that peaceful energy which had surrounded me for brief moments as a child.

* * *

Shortly after Larry and I got back together, we decided to have a baby, even though it was poor timing—he had just started a new job. We thought it would take awhile, but I became pregnant on our first try. Pregnancy brought morning sickness which lasted all day and continued for five months. When the nausea ended, severe pains in my chest began. Some nights I rolled around the bathroom floor, dagger-like pain stabbing me in the chest, while Larry slept peacefully in our bed. I was unable to ask for help and comfort, despite my terror that something was wrong with the baby. These episodes occurred frequently during the last four months of pregnancy.

Then, on March 17, 1973, after twenty-six hours of labor, an eight-pound baby boy was delivered by Caesarian-section. Unlike C-sections today, I was not awake during the delivery. And when I came out of anesthesia, I was not allowed to hold my son for several days—he'd been born jaundiced and was in an incubator.

After a one week hospitalization, we went home. The sharp pain which had plagued me those last few months of the pregnancy continued their nightly visits. Some three weeks after bringing our baby home,

47

Larry rushed me to the emergency room at 2:00 am. That night my gall bladder was removed—microscopic gallstones had been the cause of the pain during the latter part of my pregnancy. Others cared for my son, David, while I remained in the hospital for another week. Because of having a second major surgery so soon after the first, when I did come home, I couldn't properly care for my baby. It was weeks before I could lift or bathe him. My mother, my mother-in-law, Margaret, and nurses took turns caring for him. When I held David, I did not feel what I had expected to feel.

No one prepares a woman for motherhood. If she's lucky, she has a good role model in her own mother or some female relative or friend who knew what she was doing. However, the unspoken expectation is that women are born to give birth and that everything she needs is innately inside her. I'd only ever heard women speak positively of being pregnant and having a baby, so those were my expectations as well. Babysitting when I was in my teens had been my only preparation, but I'd never sat for infants—only young children six, seven, or eight years old. When confronted with a soft, squiggly, squirmy, bundle of tiny human being, my eyes glazed over, the whirling dervish in my stomach worked overtime, and my heart beat very, very fast so that breathing was shallow. By the time I got the hang of diaper-changing, it was time for a bath, which apparently terrified both me and the baby, since he screamed the entire time. I was sure I'd lose my grip and drown the child. Perhaps now, new mothers have an easier time of it, but back then we didn't talk about how hard it was to care for an infant. My fears were balanced by loving the feel of David in my arms, especially after feeding him, when he'd drift off to sleep with the sweetest expression on his face. Although desperately tired, I didn't mind waking up to feed David in the middle of the night. Those were my favorite moments, in the stillness of the dark when no one else was around but me and my child. Quite often I'd softly sing songs from *Sound of Music* and *West Side Story* or Elton John's latest hit—whatever struck my fancy.

I had wanted to do better than my parents when it came to raising a child, but I didn't even understand what they had done wrong, so how could I expect to do it better? Yes, I may have had post-partum depression—therapists later assured me I probably did. But it was compounded by being in an emotionally abusive relationship with no support system. I'd done what I thought I had wanted, but the result wasn't what I'd dreamt about as a child.

I couldn't face the truth of my situation, and even if I had been able to and known where to turn, fear of the unknown kept me stuck. Instead, I buried my feelings deep inside and when emotions surfaced, I pushed them back with food. Trying to keep peace with Larry, I remained complacent, doing the best I could with the new responsibility of mothering my child.

* * *

"David, it's my first Mother's Day," I whispered into the soft black fuzz on top of my two-month-old son's head. *Raindrops on roses and whiskers on kittens, bright copper kettles with warm woolen mittens*, I crooned as I waltzed David around his room.

"I thought I told you not to pick him up," Larry said, as he walked into David's room. "If he's fed, burped and changed then you should leave him alone. You'll spoil him."

I nodded as I rocked David gently in my arms. "He's almost asleep, Larry. I'll be right there."

Larry turned and headed downstairs. We had recently moved into a split level house in Plainview, on Long Island. I'd just turned twenty-four.

"Shh," I whispered. "Daddy doesn't have to know what we do when he's not home. Letting you cry and cry makes no sense to me. It'll be our little secret."

Placing David in his crib, I turned and walked downstairs. Thirty minutes later, I served dinner on the kitchen table.

"Larry…" I started to say, but his nose was buried in the *New York Times*. I knew better than to interrupt. After our silent meal, I went to the den and sat on the recliner. *We don't talk. We don't kiss. We don't hug. We live in the same house, but couldn't be further apart.*

Larry had become more dictatorial and at the same time more emotionally withdrawn. At this point, we'd been married four years and I was a stay-at-home mom, responsible for everything having to do with childcare and the household, except paying bills. Since I was not allowed to participate in money issues or decisions, I did not even know how to balance a checkbook.

"I need some extra money this week," I said to Larry. He was about to turn on a baseball game.

"What for?" he asked.

"I'm going to paint the kitchen cabinets." Rolling his eyes, he reached for his wallet.

He always seemed to have a comment when I asked for money, whether it was for food or something David needed. My father, too, had complained about money. Dad would scream at Mom and me if we left lights on and bellow if I were on the telephone for more than five minutes. In those days, phone users were charged by the length of the call, even if it was local. Now I wondered what it would be like to be responsible for my own welfare and not dependent on Larry for my livelihood. Each time I asked for money, I felt like Cinderella before her fairy godmother arrived.

At the same time, the women in our neighborhood seemed only interested in talking about potty training and other childcare issues, topics I cared about, certainly, but only for so long; I craved adult conversations. The loneliness and isolation I felt in my marriage followed me into motherhood. There have been several movies depicting what I call the 1950's suburban wife syndrome, but back then it wasn't even talked about. And although my experience was taking place in the early 1970's, things hadn't changed that much regarding women's roles and male and societal expectations.

Every once in awhile, the frozen me would surface and I would disagree with Larry's instructions regarding David's care. But I quickly learned that when I stood up to him, whatever remaining connection we had would fray a bit more. Yet I was unable to leave him, even when at two, he threw David across a room onto his bed. Instead, I retreated into soap operas, spending each afternoon lost in characters' pain, while David napped. As he grew older, he sat quietly and played for two hours while I continued my obsession with soaps. If he interrupted me, I'd shush him, saying we could talk when the show was over.

Just to have an outlet with other adults, I joined a bowling league. But I didn't belong there either. Once again, I didn't fit the norm—at least not the images of normal I carried in my head. Certainly it wasn't normal not to be happy about being a wife and mother—after all, hadn't

Jane Wyatt and Barbara Billingsley been perfect wives in *Father Knows Best* and *Leave it to Beaver.*

In 1973, however, Gloria Steinem, Betty Freidan, and other leaders of the women's movement began to change women's consciousness. My mother had been unusual in that she'd worked. When I was growing up, only one other friend's mother had a job outside the home. Now, women were beginning to make different choices. I'd grown up with a woman who did not enjoy marriage or motherhood, and I'd sworn I'd never be like her. Yet here I was, feeling the same way I imagine my mother had felt. Perhaps if I'd been in a healthy, loving marriage, I would have felt okay being a mom—I'll never know. Caught in that tumultuous wave of changing values and the fight for women's rights, I struggled unsuccessfully to balance my needs against the needs of a husband and child.

* * *

1975

One of the things Larry and I did enjoy doing together was going to the movies. However, everything changed when we came home after seeing the movie *Jaws*. Larry had a "mental episode," convinced the shark was coming in the window to get him. It felt so real to him that he agreed to seek professional help. During this time, his mother befriended a social worker, Mark, and sought his advice. Mark arranged for Larry to see a therapist and shortly after that, Larry and I started couples counseling. We remained in therapy for almost two years, but Larry refused to participate. I slipped deeper into depression and despair. Unable to communicate, Larry and I drifted further and further apart. In addition, my parents were not made to feel welcome in our home. Larry did not speak to them when they visited, making them, and me, uncomfortable. I'm pretty sure this played a minor role in their decision to retire to Florida.

* * *

1976

"Larry, we're invited to a party at Mark's tonight. I got a sitter for David."

"Christ, I wish my mother never introduced you two."

Eight months after David was born, Mark had "come out" to us as a gay man, so Larry wasn't threatened when I started to hang out with Mark and his friends. But Larry hated my socializing without him, so that night he agreed to come along.

At Mark's, Larry sat in the middle of the living room, arms folded across his chest, just like he did in our therapist's office, his face devoid of expression, his eyes staring straight ahead.

"It must be so difficult being married to a deaf person," a party guest said to me.

"Larry's not deaf," I replied, glancing into the living room where I'd left him a short while ago.

"He didn't respond when I talked to him," said the guest. I shrugged and walked away.

The next day, Mark called. "Why do you stay with him, Karen? I don't get it. You're smart, attractive. What gives?"

No one had ever asked me questions like this. No one had shown me a different way of thinking and looking at things. I didn't know it then, but that question was the beginning of my recovery from childhood. I told Mark I kept hoping the Larry I married would show up. But the truth was that soon after we married, his loving side disappeared. My fear of being a failure was also a factor—I wanted the marriage to work, for all our sakes. I wanted David to grow up with a mother *and* a father. I wanted to do better than my mother and father had done with me.

"You do know this isn't how a relationship is supposed to be," Mark said.

Up until that point, I'd been unable to fight for my own and David's well being. But Mark and his friends showed me another way. When I reflected on my parents' marriage and what mine had turned out to be, I knew I didn't want to live the rest of my life as miserable as they were and as miserable as I had become. It was like a glimmer of sunlight breaking through a dense fog. There was another way to be in the world and people out there who liked me just the way I was—people who didn't constantly put me down or complain about how I looked or what I said or what I did or didn't do. I wanted more of that.

* * *

January 1977

Combined, Larry and I must have had hundreds of therapy sessions, both as a couple and individually. They did not help our marriage. One night, I walked down the few stairs leading to our den, the music blaring so loudly my nerves rattled. David, now almost four, was asleep upstairs in his room on the third floor. I walked to the stereo, turned down the sound, and sat in the brown leather recliner, facing the couch. Larry threw down the *Sports Illustrated* he'd been thumbing through, and looked at me, his stormy brown eyes just slits.

"We need to talk," I said.

"We talked enough last night to last a lifetime."

The previous evening we had tried yet again to discuss our marriage, acknowledging we were both miserable, but unable to bring the conversation to a conclusion.

"We didn't resolve anything," I responded. "I've made a decision."

Larry remained silent, his eyes darting from me to the magazine to the stereo, out the window and back to me. I almost felt sorry for him. Then I heard the whisper of my friends' voices, reminding me I deserved better.

"I want a divorce," I said gently. "All our talking these last two years hasn't gotten us anywhere."

Larry's intense glare reminded me of the night I had told him I was pregnant. That night we'd fought just before going to sleep. For the first and only time in our relationship, Larry hit me. I wouldn't agree to an abortion, so he punched me in the stomach. When we'd gone to bed that night, I had a dream. *I am pregnant, standing at the window, anxious and afraid. The child in my womb is out there in the dark somewhere, crying. Unable to find it, I hold my hands over my swollen belly, confused, yet knowing I must give birth to this child.*

My stomach clenched as Larry's fingers curled into fists. He got up and stood over me, his large, almost six-foot frame casting a dark shadow.

Shrinking back in the chair, I looked up at him.

"I wasn't ready to have this child," Larry said. "You insisted. Now that we have it, we should raise it together. I don't want David growing up the same miserable way you and I did." Like a caged tiger, Larry paced back and forth.

"But he *is* growing up like we did," I said, "in a house without love."

Inside the tower of anger before me, I could still see the hunky Larry I thought I had fallen in love with almost nine years ago. In unguarded moments, I caught the mischievous glint in his eyes and remembered the Larry who looked and sounded like John Lennon singing "*I should have known better with a girl like you.*" My fingers tingled, remembering how it felt to run them through his thick, dark hair. My skin still ached for those muscular arms to wrap around me. Even though the sex had not been satisfying, I did love being held by my husband. But the cuddling had ended as the marriage began and I couldn't remember the last time I'd been in his arms.

"We've been over and over this," I said, "both in counseling and out. You wake up, go to a job you hate, come home to a family you don't seem happy to see. We both deserve more, don't we?"

I stood up. Until now, neither of us had been willing to admit defeat, neither wanted to take that last, drastic step. Larry walked back to the couch and sat down, his shoulders slumped, his eyes downcast. I caught a glimpse of the picture on the wall behind the couch: Larry's broad shoulders were wrapped around his grandfather; he was kissing the top of Poppy's bald head. *Poppy had been the one who had brought us together.*

"What will you do?" Larry asked, as I wiped my eyes.

I told him I'd been offered a job at a temple for one hundred and twenty dollars per week and that I could probably manage with that and just three hundred dollars a month alimony.

"You found a job? When did that happen? What will you do with David?"

"He'll split his time between nursery school and day care," I said. "I think you should keep the house. I'll get a small apartment."

I held my breath. The amount I mentioned was less than I needed, but it was my hope Larry could afford it and wouldn't balk at our separating. I had no idea what he earned or what our financial status was and just guessing at what my own expenses would be.

"We'll finish this tomorrow," he said as he picked up his magazine and began to thumb the pages.

The next day, Larry arrived home around 6:00 pm. His mom had taken David out earlier, so Larry and I had the house to ourselves. As we sat down to eat Larry's favorite meal, his mother's meatball recipe, I glanced at the bright yellow and white kitchen cabinets I had painted just a few months ago. Yellow was a warm, cheerful color, but it hadn't made the coldness in our house disappear.

"Larry" I started to say, but once again his nose was stuck in the newspaper and remained there for the rest of the meal. An hour later, after cleaning the kitchen, I curled up in the recliner in our den to read the mystery novel I had started the night before. Books and soap operas were my escape from the emptiness of my marriage and the suburban life I thought I'd wanted. But the words blurred on the page. My eyes roamed the room, from the entertainment center taking up one whole wall, to the brown and white sleeper couch with the rough fabric that chafed my skin. I rubbed my palm on the soft leather of the recliner. The room was all Larry. It wasn't his fault. I was incapable of speaking up for myself, even about decorating choices. Telling Larry I wanted a divorce was the first time I was aware of articulating my wants and needs out loud without crying, yelling, or manipulating to get what I wanted—or simply giving up and giving in to someone else's desires.

"Okay," Larry said, as he came downstairs and sat on the couch facing me. "You're right. We're both miserable. You take David; I'll stay in the house. I need some time to figure things out." He took out his wallet and wrote a check to cover one month.

"We'll need to make this legal, Larry."

"I know. We'll see a lawyer."

Upstairs in our room, I made a mental note to phone the rabbi to accept the position. The next day I began searching for an apartment in Queens, where I'd grown up.

Mark knew an attorney who handled family law, so the next week Larry and I went to see him. Two weeks later, we walked out of the lawyer's office with a separation agreement granting me full custody of our son. Larry had signed the papers with no argument. It was January 1977.

Later that night, I told Mark about the two-bedroom apartment

I'd found and shared how isolated I felt living in suburbia and about the looks of horror I had received from the neighborhood women when I talked about getting a job. I couldn't wait to move closer to the city, believing that urban women would be more enlightened.

But two months later, ensconced in that Queens apartment and working for the first time in four years, I felt anything but liberated. Being a single mom was the hardest and scariest thing I'd ever done. It seemed as if everything I'd wished and hoped for since I was very young was being thwarted at every turn. I'd chosen a husband who was as incapable of showing love and affection as my parents had been. David screamed nightly for his Dad. At the end of the month there wasn't enough money to put food on the table. I had no one to turn to except Mark.

But there were also some good moments. I loved David's little feet padding into my room in the morning. "Can I have graham crackers and milk, Mommy?" he would ask. I enjoyed watching him play with his matchbox cars in the living room. And the occasional snuggles during bedtime stories were heavenly. Usually, though, our evening ritual was a nightmare.

"I want my Daddy! I want my Daddy! I want my Daddy!" David wailed as he launched himself onto his brand new, big boy bed, clutching the black and white panda bear which never left his side.

"I know, honey. But you can't right now. Soon, soon you'll be able to see Daddy," I said. I walked out and left David screaming for his Daddy while I spent the next hour or so crumbled at the base of my refrigerator, crying on the phone to friends. I was puzzled by David's behavior—Larry had never been a huge part of David's day. In fact, once David became a toddler, Larry had basically ignored him.

Not much was written then about what happens to a small child when a divorce occurs, so I remained in the dark about how to handle these tantrums and how to interpret David's behavior. And just as I had done when I was a child, I misinterpreted much of what occurred between David and me. I asked Mark how to explain to a four-year-old that his father didn't want to see him.

"You don't," he replied, "at least not without risking alienating his relationship with his Dad."

* * *

56

Mothers began to arrive with their three and four-year-olds in tow, tumbling little whirlwinds of energy dashing here and there like balls in a pinball game. It was David's fourth birthday and since all his friends were in Plainview, Long Island, it made sense to host the party there. Maria (a new friend I'd met in Queens after the separation from Larry) and I were putting the last handful of helium balloons on the tables of the local restaurant.

"I can't believe how nervous I am," I said to Maria. "Carol has not returned my calls in months. I don't understand why she's been so standoffish. I hope I get a few minutes to talk to her today."

"Don't worry. I'm sure there's a reasonable explanation," said Maria, as she placed David's presents on a table next to the birthday cake.

I had tried to keep David connected to Larry's family. During the first month of our separation, Carol and Margaret had come to my apartment, but shortly thereafter, they'd stopped visiting. I still loved them and was desperate to maintain relationships, but Carol, Margaret, Grammy and Poppy had suddenly withdrawn from me, and I didn't understand why. They simply stopped communication.

As David ran from one table to another playing with his friends, Maria and I kept busy, mopping up spilled drinks, wiping a fallen child's tears, and trying to get each child's order straight while the waitress tapped her pencil on her pad, her foot keeping time to the Beatles music which blared in the background.

"Daddy," David yelled, as he made a mad dash for the door. He scrambled into his father's arms. Larry marched into the crowded room, nodding his head in my direction. Glancing behind him, I searched for Carol, seeing her through the glass window as she exited her car. As David streaked past me, shrieking, "Aunt Carol," I stood up. Carol swept him into her arms as if he were the most precious thing on Earth. Arms outstretched with longing to hold my friend, I started to walk over, but Carol's eyes looked past me as she brushed by, cold and silent. It was the first of many losses before I woke up enough so that I could make healthier choices in both friendships and relationships with men.

* * *

57

"I'm losing it," I said to Mark. "It's just not getting better. David doesn't love me. I know it. All he wants is Larry, Larry, Larry. I don't know how much more I can take."

I had wanted to minimize the changes David had to face by maintaining some familiarity in his routine. Each morning, I rose at 5:00 am, just enough time to get myself and David ready for the day. Then we had a two-hour drive from our apartment in Queens to David's nursery school on Long Island, after which I drove to my job at the temple. Although harder on me, this allowed David to keep his same friends. At the end of the day, I picked David up at school and drove back to Queens. It was 7:00 pm by the time dinner was on the table, 9:00 pm before David was asleep in bed. Staggering into my own bed around 10:00 pm, I lay sleepless most nights, worried how the divorce was affecting my son and questioning my ability to cope.

Six exhausting months later, to make things easier on myself, I started planning to move David's life closer to home. I registered him in a summer camp in Queens, hoping this would enable me to find work in Manhattan where I'd have a better chance of finding a higher paying job. But Larry had other ideas.

"Sorry," Larry informed me after I told him about camp. "I just don't have the money right now."

"But our agreement says you will pay for summer camp," I said.

"Well, I don't have it," Larry said and hung up.

Mark asked if I could take Larry to court, but I didn't have the money for that. The next day, Larry called with an offer to let David stay with him for the summer. After two months of refusing to see him and four months of visiting with David only sporadically, this was both a surprise and a godsend. I told him I'd call him back with a decision.

Tired of scraping the bottom of my purse, searching coat pockets for loose change to buy dinner, I felt humiliated and drained. In those days, I didn't have the self-esteem to assert myself to get my needs met. I was emotionally bankrupt, physically exhausted, and spiritually depleted.

"I know you're worried about how Larry will treat David, but I can't imagine it will be that awful," said Mark. "You deserve a break," he continued, after I explained Larry's offer. I agreed.

The next day I phoned to tell Larry he could have David for the summer. *Anything for some peace and quiet, some time to think.*

A week later, I drove David to Plainview and dropped him off at Larry's, grateful I would have some alone time for awhile. We agreed that I would bring David to my apartment every other weekend through the summer.

Several weeks later, Mark and I moved in together to save on expenses. Mark was concerned about Larry's reaction to me cohabitating with a gay man, but I didn't think Larry would care; he knew Mark and his sexual orientation had never been an issue before.

A short time later, Mark came home from work one night, threw his briefcase on the kitchen table, and told me he was tired of painting on such a small canvas. He had an idea for a business—he wanted to open a public relations firm to help therapists in private practice attract clients.

"We would place articles in newspapers and magazines quoting the therapists and arrange interviews on radio and television for them, where they would talk about issues," Mark explained. "Then, the people who need help with that particular issue will know where to go." He told me he could teach me what I needed to know and that with his creativity and my personality and organizational skills, we'd make a great team.

Until that moment, I never thought I'd have any other career but being a secretary. I'd gone to a two-year community college because that's where my boyfriend at the time went to school. Friends I'd grown up with had graduated from college and were now teachers or lawyers or accountants—all professionals. But I had married Larry after getting my associate degree and supported him while *he* finished college. Then David came along and there wasn't time or money for me to go back to school.

Job, career and money issues affect us all, whether we're male, female, married, single, just starting out or already established. For women, however, the path to success in business is more complex and therefore, can be more difficult. Traditionally, men have been freed from other responsibilities in order to pursue their careers. Women, on the other hand, have had to juggle career, household chores, children and relationship. Our society has undergone a major social change, where traditional roles shifted and men are participating much more in parenting and household responsibilities. I grew into adulthood before this cultural change took place. When I got married in 1969, most women were still staying home with their babies. My childhood was unusual in that my mother worked. She had to. My father's eighth grade education limited his income potential severely. Luckily, he landed a job in the post office—steady, secure, and with a good pension plan. But my background, society's expectations, the women's movement, and my own needs and desires clashed inside me during my first marriage, creating havoc and turmoil, both internally and externally.

I needed to learn several things: what would be satisfying and fulfilling to me and how to achieve balance in my life between work, family and self. The first step was to become conscious, to bring into conscious awareness the attitudes, beliefs and opinions I had about money and success.

Everyone has his or her own definition of success. For some it is financial rewards, for others it is personal satisfaction derived from work. Or it might be the ability to achieve balance. To be successful, it is helpful to be clear about one's personal, working definition of success and create a clear path to achieving it.

When I was growing up, I had no ambition other than to be a wife and mother, and to do it better than my parents had. I failed at that. Mark's business idea was my opportunity to find a new identity. Although unaware of this at the time, the ice began melting around the frozen me. My spiritual journey to find peace as well as understand and make sense of my life began and the trajectory of my life altered in that moment. It became about healing my fractured soul and growing as a person. Right around this time, I started keeping a journal—a tool which would prove to have a profound impact on my journey towards consciousness.

I sold my engagement ring for eight hundred dollars. We bought an IBM Selectric typewriter (home computers, fax machines and cell phones hadn't arrived on the scene yet), kept files in cardboard boxes in the bathtub and launched our business. That, along with my new job in Manhattan, provided enough money to support David and me. I even managed to save some money. Things were under control, so I was feeling somewhat stronger when, in early September, my lawyer suggested I take David back from Larry. I'd gotten so caught up in starting our business that I'd allowed time to slip by. Summer was gone.

"I don't think it's a good idea to move David out right now," Larry said when I phoned him later that night. "He's already started kindergarten."

"Do you really think that matters? It's only been a few weeks since school started. He will adjust."

The discussion went back and forth, but the issue of custody was never mentioned. I had the legal papers giving me custody, to which Larry had agreed with no arguments, so I thought he was just giving me a hard time. How could I have been so wrong? I told Larry I was going to pick David up the following Saturday and hung up.

* * *

Chapter 7

Losing Custody

<u>New York 1977</u>

The phone rang as I walked into my office Tuesday morning. Rushing to grab it, I answered, "Mr. Goldman's office."

An unfamiliar male voice responded, "You'd better get your son. Your husband and mother-in-law are planning to take him. I suggest you hurry."

"Who is this?" I shouted, but a click signaled that the connection had been broken.

My heart raced and my chest was so tight, my breath came in gasps. Immediately, I phoned Larry, and when I couldn't reach him, I tried his family. Over the next three days, I frantically attempted to discover David's whereabouts, finally managing to reach Larry at his office on Friday.

"I don't know what you're talking about, Karen," Larry said, after I questioned him about where David had been. "Just come tomorrow to get David like you said you would."

The warm breeze of Indian summer brushed my face as I exited the office building where I worked as Mr. Goldman's secretary. He was a Vice President at Federation Employment and Guidance Services, a large social service organization. The leaves were just beginning to turn from green to yellow, and I felt a familiar childhood sensation of coming changes. I tried to forget the disturbing phone call I'd received earlier that week and focus, instead, on David's coming home, but the fear from the warning the stranger had imparted remained curled in the pit of my stomach.

On Saturday, I pulled up to the modest, brown split-level house in Plainview—the one I had begged Larry to buy after David was born. Parking my 1969 gold Dodge Charger in front of the house, I got out and walked up the path. *It feels so awkward to have to ring my own doorbell.* Before my hand reached it, however, the door opened and a tall, thin, bald man shoved a brown envelope into my hand and shut the door in my face. Pounding the door with both fists, I shouted, "Larry, where is David? What is this? What's happening here?" There was no response.

David frequently played with our neighbor's daughter, so I ran across the lawn on a hunch he was there. Minutes later, with the soft skin of David's cheek pressed against my neck, I moved quickly towards my car, but not fast enough.

"Just a minute," Larry yelled as he tore out of the house. "You can't take him."

Ignoring Larry's shouts, I kept walking. Just as I reached to open the passenger door, he caught up to us.

"Mommy, Mommy, Mommy," David screamed, as Larry ripped my son's arms from around my neck, wrenching him away from me. Stunned and speechless, I watched Larry stride angrily back to the house with David cowering on his father's hip, straddled sideways under Larry's arm. Not wanting to traumatize my son further, I let him go. Arms empty, still warm where David had nestled just moments ago, I crumbled onto the pavement next to my car.

Slumped on the curb, I stared up at the house and felt the dream of being a wife and mother—a dream I had harbored since I was five—die. My happily-ever-after fairytale had morphed into a horror story. From the beginning, I'd known that I had made a terrible choice in husbands, but until that door slammed shut with my son behind it, I had not experienced how devastating such a choice could be and how negatively it would impact my life. However, it also became my "wake-up call," a catalyst for major internal restructuring. But that wouldn't occur until much later.

Seconds, minutes, hours later—I don't know for sure—I stood up and managed to insert the key into the car door. Sinking into the driver's seat, I wiggled the key into the ignition and turned it. As the engine roared to life, I rested my head on the steering wheel. I felt as I had many years ago when I'd been playing in the tide while jumping waves at Rockaway Beach and suddenly found myself swirling upside down underwater, caught in an undertow, not knowing which way was up or down and afraid I would drown. Shifting the gears into drive, I eased the car down the quiet, tree-lined street, the same street I had pushed David's stroller down a thousand times. *I don't know how I'm going to drive without killing myself.* Somehow, I arrived at the diner and stumbled into the booth where my friend and housemate, Mark, waited for me as we had arranged earlier that day.

Mark calmly took the papers which had been shoved into my hands and began reading. A restraining order had been issued preventing me from seeing my son. The papers alleged that I had had sex with men in front of David, as well as orgies while he was in the room. Later that night, Mark said I looked like a ghost—my face drained of color, my body slack. I felt as if my soul had left my body. Part of me was destroyed as I realized that the man I had loved and married, and had a child with, could concoct such lies, let alone convince a judge to keep me from my son.

Sitting in that diner, across from my friend, waves of emotion threatened to overwhelm me. Alternately I cried, got angry, went numb, and cried again. The room shifted out of focus. Conversations and sounds receded. I was incapable of thinking or focusing on a single thought. Years later, a therapist explained that I had gone into shock.

"How could he do this?" I asked Mark. "He never said he wanted David. I don't understand. For months after we separated, he didn't even want to see David, and now this. What am I going to do?"

"Karen," Mark said in his deep, soothing voice. "We'll figure something out. Don't worry."

As a counselor for a social services agency, Mark was used to dealing with people in crisis. Eventually, my heartbeat slowed, the sobs lessened, and objects and people in the room became visible once again.

During the excruciating drive home, my mind flip-flopped. Why had this happened to me? Closing my eyes, I leaned my head back and took a deep breath. Marriage had not given me the love I craved. And Larry had been miserable as well. Didn't we both have a right to be happy?

64

Was I so wrong? I'd given it eight years—eight years of emptiness where I felt as unloved and unwanted as I had during childhood. Finally, I'd found the courage to speak my truth and asked for a divorce, believing we would all be better off, including Larry. But the consequence of speaking my truth was losing my son.

I wasn't sure of anything at that moment except that on some deep level, I had failed at the very thing I had wanted most. And that my choices and actions had perhaps caused my child as much, if not more, harm than my parents' actions had caused me. Faced with an ugly custody battle with a man who carried enough anger and hatred to crush me and devastate our son, the question which would haunt me for years to come gurgled into my consciousness: *What is wrong with me?* Aside from Mark, I was alone. I felt a huge, gaping hole in the center of my body—a dark abyss into which I would implode—were it not for a thin lifeline, a safety net I felt with Mark. And safe was a new feeling.

* * *

October 1977

After I had been served with the restraining order, fear, along with shame and humiliation, became as much a part of me as my skin. I immediately consulted with three different attorneys.

As long as I lived with a gay man, I stood no chance of winning custody, they assured me. Even if I moved out on my own, I would probably lose. We knew Larry had lied to a judge when he'd said I'd slept with men while David was in the room. It didn't matter that it was unfair. What mattered was that the case would be argued in conservative Nassau County and the odds were that I would lose, they said.

"How could Larry have convinced a judge to issue that restraining order?" I asked one attorney. "I was never contacted. No one asked whether I'd had orgies with David in the room. No one questioned whether that or the other allegations were true."

"I don't know. The judge must have been convinced of Larry's veracity," he said.

Without letting me know, Larry had hooked up with my former friend Ellen sometime during the summer. She'd been married to Larry's best friend, Robert. They were part of the group of couples who used to gather monthly to sing and play canasta. But Robert had been killed in an automobile accident shortly after Larry and I separated. And not long after that, Ellen had stopped communicating with me. Now I knew why.

I ranted to friends. I told the lawyers about the time Larry hit me when I was pregnant, obviously angry about becoming a father. Why would he suddenly want his child now? They heard about the time Larry had thrown David across the room when he was two. Still, they said that because Larry was now part of a family and I was not, I would probably lose custody.

"Maybe you should consider moving out on your own; you might have a chance at winning," Mark said one night after dinner.

"I've thought about it and talked it over with each of the attorneys. If I thought that would ensure me winning, I would. But they say there are no guarantees."

Sleep eluded me. Concentration was difficult. I felt like a gutted fish. *I'm not sure I am emotionally capable of raising a child. Maybe this is happening for a reason. Maybe I am not good for David. Ellen is stable, even if Larry isn't. She is a good mother, a decent person. She has three boys of her own; I am godmother to one of them. David will be in good hands with her.* I clung to Mark like a drowning woman clutching a life jacket.

Despite the good feelings I was developing as a result of our business, deep inside I remained convinced something was fundamentally wrong with me and that David was, perhaps, better off without me. Alongside that truth, however, lurked another darker truth—that part of me wanted to abdicate responsibility. Yet I was scared to leave David in Larry's hands. Since I wasn't able to articulate these feelings, no one could help me sort out my conflicting thoughts and see things more clearly.

"Karen, I can't tell you what to do," Mark said. "No one can."

My therapist said the same thing. Only I could decide.

With Ellen there, Larry's impact on David won't be so bad. Where will I get the money to fight a long, protracted legal battle? My parents certainly don't have it. And I'm being told I'll lose anyway. Oh God, I feel so hopeless. How can I not fight for my child? But I'll lose. I'll be in debt forever. I'll never get the money. What about our business? How will all this affect it? I have to fight. I don't want to fight. I can't fight. For eight long months, these thoughts raged inside me until I thought I'd go mad. Finally, I caved.

"Mark," I said one night. "I've gone from being a petite brunette weighing one hundred twenty pounds to a one hundred seventy-pound blob with gray hair. I've been diagnosed with colitis. Three attorneys can't be wrong. Even though it feels like I'm giving up, I'm not going to fight Larry in court."

So, on May 26, 1978, Larry was awarded sole custody of David, and I became a non-custodial parent with visitation rights. I was twenty-nine years old. In those days, a father getting custody of a child was relatively unheard of—and joint custody was not as yet a common resolution for divorcing couples.

The self-hatred I'd felt as an adolescent paled in comparison with the venom I directed at myself now. Unable to stand up to Larry, I hadn't protected David from Larry's emotional abuse. Deep down inside, I knew I was a bad mother, that I was flawed as a female, that I didn't enjoy sex, that I'd had a miserable pregnancy, that I hadn't been able to give birth naturally, that I didn't feel an automatic love for my baby the day he was born. Of course I was conflicted about my ability to raise him.

Now I understand that it is normal to have moments when you don't feel loving towards your child, but I didn't grasp that then. I didn't know how post-partum depression can influence your feelings—it wasn't that I didn't love my baby. I just didn't feel what I'd heard and read other women describe when they gave birth. In addition, I didn't have a clue what love was; that there are different kinds of love; that just because people behave in certain ways, doesn't necessarily mean they love or don't love you. Coupled with that confusion was guilt for wanting a career and because part of me was relieved when David was gone that summer. I wanted him back because it was the right thing to do, but I didn't know how to parent a child who didn't seem to love me *and* own a business *and* heal my childhood wounds.

Becoming a non-custodial parent altered my maternal DNA. Instead of being the one who made sure David brushed his teeth, dressed properly, ate a good breakfast, and got to school on time, I became a weekend activities counselor. Losing custody carved a hole in my heart where my son was supposed to be that remained unfilled for the next eighteen years.

* * *

Chapter 8

"Mommy, how could you leave me?"

One Friday afternoon, several months after the custody decision, David trudged out of Larry's house with his backpack clutched tightly in his hands. Slowly he climbed into my car.

"Hi, sweetie," I said. "I'm so happy to see you."

"Hi," he mumbled, staring down at his sneakers.

Turning towards him as we drove away, I said, "Guess what? We're going into Manhattan, a place called Greenwich Village to see *A Hard Day's Night* and *Help*."

A small smile crept across David's face. He'd been listening to the Beatles his entire life. The 8th Street Theater was packed and we barely managed to find two seats together when the credits rolled and the music came on. "*Help, I need somebody. Help. Not just anybody.*" The people around us giggled and I turned to see David bouncing up and down in his seat as he sang along with the movie. Larry was a Beatles fanatic, so David knew the words to all the songs. I smiled and pulled him close. He looked up and smiled back.

That was one of our better moments. Mostly, though, Saturday after every other Saturday, a similar pattern presented itself. I planned an outing I thought might be fun, David would be uncommunicative.

Transitioning into part-time mommy was not easy for either David or me. Mark and I lived in a one-bedroom apartment in Rego Park, Queens. We put an extra mattress in the bedroom when David came

68

to stay. Looking back with a distance of decades, I recognize I might have made better choices. Children need their own space in a home, a place where they know their toys and clothing can be found. David did not have that at our place. We lived a somewhat bohemian lifestyle, but David was never exposed to Mark's homosexuality or any of my attempts at sexual relationship with other men. Since I'd been introduced to sexuality at a very young age, I was not about to let that happen to my child. Instead, David was shown a new world. Literature, self-help, philosophy, and psychology books lined the walls of our living room and bedroom. Soft pillows were scattered around the rooms. The colors were earth tone shades of brown and gold. At the time I saw nothing wrong with the situation. I thought flexible mealtimes and some chaos, rather than strict structure was a good thing.

In addition to the cozy sleeping arrangements, Mark and I ran our business from every available space in the apartment. Sales calls were conducted while seated on a chair outside our kitchen where the only telephone hung on the wall. Cardboard boxes with client files were heaped in the bathtub and the typewriter sat on a desk piled high with papers.

When I initially left Larry, I'd rented a two-bedroom apartment, with a bedroom for me and one for David. But I couldn't afford the upkeep. My choice to room with Mark was right for me, but in hindsight, we should have moved into my apartment, not his. We'd chosen his because it was cheaper, but mine had two bedrooms and David would have had his own room. But I had yet to learn to balance my needs against the needs of others, especially my child's.

David and I, though, did manage to have precious moments like the one in the movie theater. Sometimes we did things alone, sometimes with Mark. I was trying to create a "family." Mark, a gay male, also wanted a sense of family, so he, too, made efforts with David. He attempted dream therapy, hoping to move David past the trauma of the divorce. At breakfast, we would share our dreams and draw pictures depicting them. Afterwards, we'd practice yoga together. But often, David played alone, while Mark and I worked or talked about adult things.

One Sunday afternoon, we took David to a free Elton John concert in Central Park. We sat in the middle of the great lawn, surrounded by thousands of screaming fans, and watched and listened to Elton John mesmerize his audience with "Crocodile Rock" and "Danny's Song."

After the performance, David wrapped his arms tightly around my neck.

"Honey, it's time to go back to Dad," I said.

"Okay," said David, his brown eyes sad.

Like other Sunday nights, we drove up to Larry's house and David scrambled out of the car without a backward glance. Even if there were glimpses of connection during our weekend together, they disappeared during the ride back to Plainview. How could I have expected a little boy to grasp the dynamics of a bitter divorce and the subsequent behavior of the parents who should have put aside their own needs to care for their son? David was in an impossible situation and, not knowing what had really occurred between Larry and me, perhaps made the only choice possible for him—his father.

* * *

1981

Three years after losing custody, I attended a parent/teacher conference at David's school. Earlier that week I had phoned to connect with David's teacher and found out about the conferences. Larry called later that night, screaming into the phone that I wasn't legally allowed to do what I had done. I had no parental rights and needed his permission prior to participating in events such as these.

Each time something like this happened—and there were many—I was reminded that I wasn't a "real" parent anymore and could no longer parent David in ways I felt would benefit him. More and more, I felt like a failure as a woman and a mom. The fact that Larry did not inform me about school issues or problems David was having didn't factor into my feelings. I blamed myself completely.

I had barely adjusted to being a non-participating parent, when, several months later, Larry told me David was in counseling and his therapist wanted to see me. Over the course of several individual sessions with David's therapist, I learned a bit about David's life with Larry and Ellen. David wasn't just acting out with Mark and me; he was also unhappy living with them. I had assumed they had the perfect marriage—the one I'd always wanted. I also believed that David was only miserable when he was with Mark and me. The therapist said the opposite was true. Larry and Ellen fought often and Larry was unkind to Ellen's three children. Anger and tension permeated their household, just as it had Larry's and mine. All the kids were acting out and having problems in school.

At that point, I decided to seek the therapist's help. As David's advocate, if he understood what Larry had done and how he had gained custody, perhaps he could help me forge a connection with my son. When I told him about the false allegations in the restraining order stating that I'd had sex with men while David was in the same bed, and that orgies had taken place in front of the child, he was flabbergasted. I could tell he wasn't sure whether to believe me or not. I could only assume Larry had told David, the therapist, and others, his version of the truth about me.

* * *

During this same time frame, Mark and I built a business. Six months after we began, both of us were able let go of our jobs and work at the business full time. Our first large client was a group physician practice and my initial assignment was to conduct a survey to determine how people felt about their family physicians. The subsequent marketing plan we implemented created a successful launch for our client and thus, our business was successfully launched as well. Several additional medical clients came on board as a result of our work, and my self-esteem with regard to work grew with each success. Instead of typing someone else's reports and recommendations, I was creating my own. I had a career rather than a job.

Over the next few months I saw David's therapist a few times and during one of the sessions, I shared my distress over the lack of connection with David. He suggested I might be too focused on the business—that I wasn't paying as much attention to David as I should in our times together. He was right. My energy *was* focused on the business. Its success was fueling a newfound sense of self. But the issues went deeper than that, and, unfortunately, that therapist wasn't able to provide helpful insight. Instead, I felt blamed for creating the problem in the first place (by asking Larry for a divorce) and then contributing to David's problems

71

by being a businesswoman rather than a parent. He never addressed Larry's and Ellen's attitudes and how those attitudes might be affecting David's behavior towards me.

Increasingly concerned about David and how he was coping with his life in Plainview, I asked David's therapist at one point, if David would be better off with me, since he was so unhappy. But the therapist said no, and at the time, I accepted his opinion, even if I didn't understand it. I contemplated trying to regain custody, but came to believe that if David's therapist thought he was better off with Larry, than perhaps he was. Deeply conflicted, I was torn between David's misery and my doubts about being a good mom. The conflicts were compounded by my growing sense of accomplishment as a businesswoman.

The truth was, I was happier when David wasn't there. The emotional distance between us made me feel like a freak of nature—*don't all children automatically love their mothers?* Once more, unable to deal with my feelings, I numbed myself. As a result, although I did not realize it while it was occurring, I proceeded to lose David's childhood. I wasn't invited to his birthday parties. Nor was I asked to watch David play sports. I never got to help him with his homework, put a bandage on a skinned knee, or talk to him about girls when he reached adolescence.

It was only after years of therapy that I allowed myself to process the grief associated with those losses. Until then, I had done whatever I could to numb the pain. Like when the painter molested me or my father or Larry verbally abused me, I became the leaf frozen in the glacier ice. Sometimes, though, emotions broke through, and when they did, the pain was so overwhelming, I contemplated suicide. Powerless to change the situation, and unable to speak up for myself with Larry, Ellen or David's therapist, it was easier to succumb to doubts about my mothering or tell myself David didn't need me anyway—he had Ellen. The resulting shame was so pervasive, I chose instead to focus on something that made me feel good about me—our business and the spiritual exploration it sparked.

* * *

Here's how it worked. Mark was "the creative" part of the business. He designed the marketing, advertising, and PR campaigns which turned into media interviews for our clients. My responsibilities were to conduct new business calls, maintain client relations, manage the finances, and handle media relations. When I'd left Larry, I'd had to learn about money—how to keep a checkbook, make and stick to a budget, and pay bills. Although not very good in math, I was exceptional with details, which served me well in my administrative capacity in the business.

Despite my vast responsibilities, Mark saw the business as his. In his mind, he was the creator and boss, and I was just supposed to follow instructions. Mark was brilliant, but his mind flew in so many directions, it was hard to track his thoughts. I became a bridge between him and our clients. But he didn't see it that way, and for many years, neither did I. I'd been so grateful for his support during the divorce/custody battle and for wanting my help to start the business, that I ignored other problems. The fact that he'd given me this business opportunity overrode the negative aspects of our relationship.

Although Mark was vastly different than other men I'd been involved with in that he was a good listener and opened my eyes to new ways of seeing things, I still gave him all the power in our relationship. With Larry, my life had been emotionally empty, with no communication and unsatisfying and unfulfilling sex. Mark's friendship was different from anything I had previously experienced. He was brilliant, and conversations were scintillating and exciting. He could quote from a variety of sources and was knowledgeable about many subjects. Mostly, though, we talked about ourselves—our painful childhoods, what we wanted for ourselves, what we dreamed about, and how to achieve those goals. I'd never had anyone I could talk to about these things. With Carol, we'd talked about girl stuff—basically boys. My parents never talked about feelings, emotions, dreams or goals. So a whole world opened up to me in the gift of my friendship with Mark. What I couldn't foresee was how I would end up feeling about him and how he would end up manipulating and controlling me. I was still the complacent, compliant, don't-you-dare-cause- a-controversy partner. The dichotomy of my newly found self-confidence from business success on one hand, and beaten down feeling from criticisms on the other, made me feel schizophrenic.

Looking back, my lack of action in this hurtful dynamic was unhealthy, but not so surprising. I was not physically beaten, but Mark could be quite critical and dogmatic, so I still felt subservient and stuck. If I had pulled my head out of the sand and allowed myself to acknowledge what was really happening, I would have had to leave yet another relationship and give up the career that was giving me so much self-confidence. And since that was too painful to contemplate, I denied my reality once more. And at that time, the good I was receiving from my connection with Mark far outweighed the negative.

At the same time, I sought ways to ease my inner turmoil. In addition to self-help books, I began reading religious and spiritual works from a wide range of disciplines. I explored a number of paths, seeking the same kind of solace I'd found as a young child lighting Chanukah candles. I tried attending a few Jewish services, but without understanding the language, I didn't feel connected to the religion at all.

Mark, although Jewish, had been seeking spiritual comfort in church. He told me about an Episcopal Church he'd discovered and one Sunday I accompanied him. The congregants were asked to kneel for the Lord's Prayer. Unexpectedly, I knew the words to this prayer by heart, although I'd never been in a church before. As I spoke the words, I felt bathed in a soft white light, as if I'd slipped into a warm tub on a chilly day. But over the next few months, certain words in the liturgy caused me to stumble. When I'd started to work in our business full time, I began reading a wide variety of subjects to make up for my lack of formal education. I'd just completed a biography of Gandhi. I could not possibly participate in a religion which believed someone like Gandhi could not enter heaven or that there was only one true path to God. At that point, I began to separate Jesus' teachings, which I loved, from the dogma and doctrines one receives in church.

Despite Mark's beseeching me to continue attending church with him, for once I listened to my inner voice and stopped going. Instead, I read self-help books and spiritual texts, looking for a path which better suited my needs, still longing for a connection to that calm energy I'd encountered when I was eight. Years later, I came to believe that there are many paths to God and that inner peace comes from making the attempt to connect with Spirit—the specific path does not matter. But back then neither Mark nor I found our way. He continued to attend Church services, but still hungered for deeper healing, constantly seeking out new therapies. And in the 1980's, personal growth opportunities abounded.

* * *

One evening in late fall, 1981, I barely noticed the gold and red leaves just beginning to drift outside the kitchen window. Elbows deep in warm, sudsy water, I turned my head slightly, watching Mark make his way through a stack of papers on the dining room table.

"I don't know what's wrong," I said. "I just don't feel right."

"Don't be silly, Karen. There's nothing wrong with you," said Mark. "The EST training is the best thing that's ever happened to us. I just don't understand you anymore."

Watching him out of the corner of my eye, I saw his brow furrow, the corners of his mouth turn town, his shoulders hunch—warning signs not to let him know how I was really feeling.

"I guess you're right. Things have been great," I said, which is what I knew he wanted to hear.

For two months we'd been attending the New York Center of the national EST organization, yet another attempt to heal our broken selves. But unlike Mark, I thought something was wrong with the people we'd met, especially the leaders. I sensed Mark and I would be damaged—I wasn't sure how—if we remained involved with this group. I also knew if I shared this with Mark, he would discount my feelings, be furious and withdraw from me—a reaction I could not emotionally afford.

In the training, we had been taught that our minds would try to trick us with thoughts about wanting to leave and were told to call the Center if that happened. But I had resisted that rule, which was odd since I almost always followed instructions. My experience as a small child in the green chair had taught me to do what I was told to do. Deep inside, I believed my concerns were justified, but since I seemed to be the only one who felt this way out of hundreds of people who had completed the training, I didn't trust myself.

I wanted to talk with Mark, but he had changed. Unlike the doubt I'd experienced since the first lecture we'd attended, Mark was enthusiastic from the start. He insisted it was normal to be apprehensive and parroted back the message that had been expressed over and over during meetings: that because the training was so different, and because growth was never comfortable, it was expected that participants would resist EST's messages. The training was designed to help people overcome their shortcomings

75

by exposing negative thought patterns. And that certainly couldn't be done with ease and comfort. It was bound to be confrontational and difficult. But I knew what I felt was more than discomfort, even if I couldn't articulate why. That first night, my intuition had screamed at me, *Get out*, but I hadn't listened.

The shrill ring of the phone interrupted my musings. Grabbing a dishcloth to dry my hands, I hurried to answer it.

"Hello? Oh, hi Linda...No, you aren't disturbing us. Yes, I'm fine...No, I wasn't planning to come tonight...I know it's important to follow through after the weekend seminars, but, I'm...hmmm. Maybe you're right. I guess I'm just afraid and once I get there, I'll be fine...okay, I'll see you at eight o'clock. And thanks, Linda, I appreciate your concern."

I hung up the phone and walked over to tell Mark I'd changed my mind. Looking up from his papers, he turned his lean frame around so he could see me, and smiled.

"That's great. I really want you with me on this. I'm sure this is what we've been looking for all these years. Everything's going to be just wonderful," he said. "You'll see."

I promised to give it everything I had.

The sun was beginning to set behind the neat row of apartment buildings in Rego Park, the quiet neighborhood where we lived in Queens. I rose and walked back to the kitchen to finish cleaning up remains from our dinner. Chewing my lower lip, I thought perhaps my earlier fears were a bit paranoid. Mark, with his vast experience in counseling and training, would certainly know if these processes were damaging. And how could so many people who seemed so ordinary be wrong? Linda was right, it was just my mind. I remembered how I'd agonized over the decision not to fight for custody of David. And how painful the years following that decision were—my mind in constant turmoil—the voices battling inside my head. A day didn't go by when I didn't think about David and question whether I'd made the right choices. In this crisis, I was in that same mind set, the one which had caused me so much pain before—perhaps it was once again trying to sabotage me.

The tension that had sizzled between Mark and me throughout dinner eased once I decided to attend the session. I thought back to what Mark had shared the night we went to our first lecture. There had been fifty, maybe seventy-five people there and two enthusiastic, confident, self-assured guest leaders at the front of the room. Both were well dressed—the man in a dark blue suit, starched white shirt and light gray tie, the woman in a stylishly cut black suit, gray silk blouse and low-heeled black pumps. Simple pearl stud earrings and a choker completed her ensemble. They spoke as if they knew what they were talking about. Both had been successful in their careers, yet had had one disastrous relationship after another. But once they finished the training and began attending sessions at The Center, their lives had turned around. Now they were seminar leaders, happily sharing the gift of the training with others. Mark turned to me and said, "This is what's been missing in my life—they have what I need to feel successful."

I finished putting the last dish away and wandered back to our cozy living room, where Mark had settled comfortably on the soft, brown futon. Sitting next to him, I tucked my legs up underneath me and gazed at the large wall lined with books. Normally, the serenity of the room settled me, but that night, my insides churned. I didn't know how to analyze what was happening. Was it normal for me to feel afraid? Could I be right and everyone else wrong? That was hard to believe. Instead, I convinced myself that I was crazy. From the time I was a small child, I had felt different. Other children played together with an ease and comfort I didn't feel. I was an outsider, never quite belonging, even when I was asked to join the activities. At home, I'd felt the same way. An only child, I believed my parents never really wanted me—that I didn't belong.

Quite often I was told how pretty I was, with my black curly hair and sparkly hazel eyes. But only I knew how ugly I felt. And at that point in my life, even though I'd lost all the weight I had gained during my marriage to Larry and was slim and attractive at thirty-two, I still believed I was ugly and felt confused when complimented. I'd had enough therapy to know that being molested had contributed to my poor self-image. My mother and father's inept parenting skills were also part of it. But thus far, I had not healed enough to trust my intuition. If I felt one way and people around me another, I had to be wrong.

My poor sense of self led to a constant search for something to make me okay. I hadn't connected to Judaism and Christianity hadn't worked either. For now, Mark was that something, and I wasn't about to let EST interfere with that connection. I thought back to when I'd first met Mark. He was lanky, about six feet tall, with curly brown hair and huge, brown, puppy-dog eyes. My mother-in-law had brought Larry and me to a lecture Mark was presenting (this occurred just after Larry's *Jaws* episode), and shortly thereafter, Larry began seeing the therapist Mark had referred him to.

The night we met, Mark was addressing a large audience, and his anchorman voice hypnotized me. Funny and charming, he had an intensity which drew people in. Being with Mark was like coming home to a place I had only dreamt about. During the legal battle with Larry, Mark's emotional support and guidance saved me. He was a lifeboat, and I had collapsed into it, letting him row me away to a new life.

But my self-doubts and need for constant reassurance soon began to wear on the relationship. The loss of my son had exacerbated my already low opinion of myself. Meeting new people had never been easy, but after losing David, I dreaded the moment I'd be asked, *Do you have children?* I didn't know how to answer: *Yes, but he doesn't live with me. No, not anymore.* But then they would think he was dead. Yet, that's how I felt—like I didn't have a child anymore.

Mark grew less tolerant as time passed. The more I craved closeness, the more distant and judgmental he became. When he'd had enough, he threatened to leave, so I promised to change. That's when I had begun therapy again, reading self-help books, and participating in women's groups while devoting the rest of my time and energy to fulfilling Mark's needs. Early on I learned to acquiesce to his demands, believing that he knew what was best for me and that he would never willingly or intentionally hurt me. This mode of operating kept things peaceful between us.

Our friendship had been struggling along for four years when Mark found The Center and convinced me EST contained all the tools we needed to heal. We had completed the two weekend seminars and had been attending weekly meetings regularly until the night I expressed my reluctance to attend.

That night, after taking the subway into Manhattan, we grabbed a cab for the quick ride to the Center. As we walked in, I scanned the cavernous room filled with men and women from all walks of life. Young, old, white collar, blue collar, all seeking answers to the feelings of hopelessness that pervaded their lives.

Sitting back in my seat, I shivered despite the heat spewing from the radiator just behind me, determined not to judge or criticize what I heard. The seminar leaders, poised and confident, were talking about space and how energy affects it. For example, we can fill space with negative, uncomfortable energy, or we can fill it with love. It's important to be aware of the energy we bring to a room and how it affects others.

I didn't disagree with what the leaders were saying. But I did disagree with the methods used to convey the messages. Sleep deprivation and starvation were part of the process. I had been blindly following Mark's advice and suggestions about how to heal myself for years, but now everything in me resisted. Something was shifting, but I was uncomfortable with the change. It would be several more years before I learned to act on my intuitions. That night, I sat back as Mark sat blissfully beside me, seemingly mesmerized.

I must be nuts, I thought, as I looked around the room. Everyone listened with beaming faces, eyes fixed, staring at the stage with rapt attention. Although I was deeply disturbed by EST and its teachings, I chose to shut up and pretend, keeping my doubts to myself.

Mark and I remained involved with EST for almost two years and nearly lost our business as a result. Our focus became recruiting people for the training rather than recruiting new clients for ourselves. There are those who believe EST was a cult. Indeed, several years later, after we extricated ourselves from The Center and began to pull our lives and business back together, we learned of others who felt the training had been harmful in some way. The combination of our EST experience and a recession which hit New York during 1982 and 1983 put us in a crisis. There were times we only had a quarter in our pockets and friends would step up and feed us. We lived on tuna fish and spaghetti. Sometimes I didn't have train fare to get out to Long Island to see David.

My pattern when things don't go as I expect them to is to become filled with despair and hopelessness. I shut down and give up, not wanting to feel the failure and frustration—I want to escape. I needed to come to terms with reality—the business was not making enough money to pay our bills, and I felt responsible for fixing it. And since it was "Mark's" business, I felt compelled to get a job.

* * *

My head peeked out of the sand enough times to begin to notice Mark's frequent criticism of my efforts. If something went wrong, I got blamed. I also began to admit that I didn't enjoy spending time with my son anymore, a feeling which threatened to erode whatever self-love I'd managed to attain thus far. After all, what kind of mother doesn't want to be with the child she had given birth to?

Since the business did not bring in enough money to support us, and since I wasn't sure about my working relationship with Mark, I accepted a job as PR assistant to a senior vice president in Chemical Bank's public relations department. The offices were located on Park Avenue, across from Citicorp. The lobby atrium was filled with greenery which surrounded the round, white metal tables with lattice tops. Mark would bring work pertaining to the few clients we had retained, and at lunchtime we went over my responsibilities. He basically outlined how to do my job at the bank. I had confidence in my administrative skills but not in my ability to handle creative aspects such as writing press releases, articles, brochures and the like.

In addition, my boss was an active alcoholic, making things even more difficult. Luckily, I had started to attend Al-Anon and Adult Children of Alcoholics meetings. One night, shortly after we disengaged from the EST organization, Mark brought home what he called a "laundry list of characteristics" people develop when growing up in an alcoholic home (his mother was an alcoholic). The list included insights like, "We guess at what normal is," and "We get guilt feelings when we stand up for ourselves." I identified with many of the characteristics, even though my parents did not drink. Mark and I both began attending meetings. In those rooms, I heard stories of childhoods much worse than mine, but the effects on the child were similar although with symptoms of varying degrees. Slowly, as a result of the twelve-step programs, I began to change. Slogans such as "Let Go and Let God," "Keep the Focus on Yourself," "Keep it Simple," and "One Day at a Time" taught me valuable lessons I hadn't learned in childhood. The slogans and other philosophies helped me negotiate my days with fewer emotional reactions and more inner strength. Gaining an understanding of alcoholic behavior also helped me deal with my new boss.

The job at Chemical Bank lasted a year and a half, after which I worked for Goodwill Industries as marketing director for six months. By that time, I was more comfortable with the creative aspects of public relations and could write brochures and releases without Mark's help. In other words, I could perform the duties of my job on my own, with my own knowledge and skill level—a major turning point in my effort to build self-esteem.

I'd reached a milestone of sorts. I was trying to evaluate whether to continue working for someone else or go back into business with Mark. At the same time, I began to take responsibility for my own behavior, recognizing when I was responsible and when someone else was, rather than automatically blaming myself when things went wrong. Learning what works and what doesn't, and when to make necessary changes were additional valuable tools. To do this, I had to recognize what I was feeling and thinking and to communicate in a healthy manner. As a child, I hadn't learned those skills. Instead, I'd been terrified of people's reactions to what I said or did, so I didn't say or do much of anything. My desperation to be liked made me fearful of saying or doing something that might cause someone to not like me.

Still, I had trouble being fully conscious and aware while traveling on my spiritual path, discovering who I was and what I was about, and fitting all that into corporate life. I learned I couldn't pretend to be someone I wasn't at work. And being myself at work was getting me in trouble, although it was helping me feel better about myself. Learning how to balance these two things still escaped me.

Around this same time, Mark met John, another gay man who had joint custody of his eight-year-old daughter. Our business wasn't making much money; Mark was busy writing a play; and my salary could not cover our expenses. John invited us to live with him in his large, two-bedroom apartment in Stuyvesant Town, located on 14th Street and Avenue C in Manhattan.

This was towards the end of 1983. I was reluctant to make the move, but sensed Mark would go without me if I didn't agree. So there I was, a divorced heterosexual woman living with not one, but two gay men. David still came for weekend visits and seemed to enjoy visiting Manhattan a bit more than Queens. It was quite a lifestyle change for him to shift from conservative Nassau County suburbia to the more

81

liberal city life of Manhattan.

David still made faces when I picked him up at Larry's, and I still struggled with my conflicting feelings toward him. When I asked questions, he responded with one-word answers or a shrug of his shoulders. Mostly, he kept to himself and treated Mark's and my efforts to engage him in conversation as an intrusion. Years later I would learn he behaved this way with everyone, but at the time, as was my wont, I thought it was my fault. The way we interacted reminded me of the dynamics between Larry and me. I tried everything I could think of to connect with David, but nothing worked. It seemed like he blamed me for the divorce and had chosen his father over me.

I've since learned that Larry's actions and David's subsequent behavior towards me follow the signs of parental alienation, but at the time, I didn't know how to interpret what was going on. According to the Parental Alienation Association (PAAO) website, symptoms of parental alienation may include children showing sudden negative changes in their attitude towards a parent, appearing uneasy around the target parent (resorting to one-word answers), failing to engage openly in conversations as they previously have done, refusing the other parent access to medical and school records, schedules, or extra-curricular activities, false allegations of sexual abuse, or displaying attitudes which give children the impression that having a good time on a visit will hurt the custodial parent.

David and I met all those criteria. But that criterion was unknown to me back then, so the way I managed my feelings regarding my relationship with David was to focus on my own healing. I contemplated leaving New York to start over. By that time, I'd convinced myself I was no good for David. If I removed myself from his life, he would be better off. But it certainly wasn't an altruistic decision; I felt as if my sanity was at stake; shame and guilt were eating away at my soul. Deep inside, I believed everyone was better off without me, but I wasn't aware of those feelings on a conscious level yet. They simply manifested in depression and suicidal thoughts.

Our custody agreement allowed David to spend a few weeks with me each summer, but I only remember one particular summer vacation. In July 1984, Mark, John and his daughter, and David and I went to a remote island in Northern Maine. The instructions to get there had come on two, single-spaced typewritten pages. From the first night when we couldn't get our tent up, to getting lost and arriving late to the spot where we were to meet the boat which would take us to the island, the trip was a complete disaster. We had to climb up a steep embankment in the dark, carrying groceries and equipment while making sure the two children did not fall into the lake. When a spider crawled across my face in the outhouse, I nearly had a nervous breakdown.

But with the light of day the next morning, the green landscape against the azure water calmed me. It was my first experience with Nature as Spirit.

David remained withdrawn no matter how we tried to encourage him to participate in activities. But with the serenity of the island came clarity. I realized that I needed to take a giant step forward in my healing. After batting my head against the unrelenting solidarity of Larry, Ellen, and David for years, I still didn't have an acceptable relationship with my son. By removing myself, I was sure he would stop feeling as if he had to choose between them and me. And I, in turn, could move forward with my own life.

* * *

September 1984

"I'm not sure whether I'm right or not," I told Mark one night, several weeks after we returned home from Maine. "But if I move away, things might be easier for David. Would you consider leaving New York and moving to the West Coast?"

Our business still hadn't recovered from the EST interruption and the recession, so Mark wasn't earning any money. We were living on my salary and John's generosity. Mark asked where I wanted to move.

"Ever since I was seventeen, I've wanted to go to California. I've never been anywhere but New York, the Bahamas, and Florida," I said.

After some research, Mark said he thought Oregon would be a better place to begin again. I wasn't sure, but he said Oregon sounded beautiful. Two rivers embraced Portland on either side. The ocean lay two hours in one direction; Mount Hood decorated the sky two hours the other way. Its economy was growing and, since it was smaller than New York, if we decided to launch our business there, we had a better chance of success.

Mark had a hunch about Oregon and, trusting him, I said okay.

"Don't you think David still needs you?" Mark asked. "Even if he only gets you part time?"

"No," I replied. It had been almost six years and I still felt rejected and unloved by my child. I told Mark I didn't think my presence in David's life affected him one way or the other.

"I'm being torn apart inside. If I stay, I'll explode."

Colitis still plagued me, I was overweight yet again, and could see no solution to the problems I faced. I talked myself into believing I needed a drastic external change. Mark said he'd support whatever I wanted to do.

That Friday night, after a silent ride from Plainview to our apartment, I sat David down in our living room.

"Mark and I are moving away," I said.

His eyes grew wide and he asked where.

"A place called Portland, Oregon," I said. I told him it was on the other side of the country and that he would visit on holidays and during the summer. Reaching over, I hugged David tight to my chest. This time he returned the hug. When he asked why I was moving, I explained that I needed time to take care of myself.

On Sunday night, Mark drove to Plainview while I sat in the backseat, eleven-year-old David snuggled up against me. When we arrived at Larry's house, I got out with him. As he walked towards the front door, David turned and said, "Mommy, how could you leave me?"

I stooped in front of David and looked him straight in the eyes.

"Someday I hope you'll understand this, but right now I know it's hard," I said. "Don't ever doubt for one second how much I love you."

I watched as David turned and ran into the house. I could see Ellen waiting in the hall as the door closed behind my son.

Sliding into the front passenger seat, I leaned my head against the side window. Mark reached over and rubbed my shoulder. He made a U-turn and headed back to the freeway. I stared out the window, the blackness of night broken only by the lights on the Long Island Expressway, my dry eyes hurting from unshed tears.

* * *

"Well, that's everything, Mark," I said, as I closed the lid on the suitcase. "We're as ready as we'll ever be."

We had sold everything we owned except our computer, our business portfolio, family photos, and clothing. The old Volvo we had purchased last year, beat-up and dented so no one would steal it, was already stuffed and awaited us on Second Avenue and Avenue C.

"Let's take a last drive around the city," Mark said. "Portland is a long way away and who knows when we'll get back to New York."

Mark grabbed the suitcase and walked to the elevator. I took one last look around the apartment, turned and walked out. John remained in his bedroom, unable to watch us go.

The car filled with silence as we headed uptown.

After awhile, I said, "I am really glad to be getting out of this city." We were stuck in bumper-to-bumper traffic in my favorite part of Manhattan.

"I agree," said Mark. "Portland has only two hundred and fifty thousand people in the metropolitan area, quite a difference from eight million."

We headed towards the George Washington Bridge, which took us to New Jersey, where we caught Interstate 80. Several days later, after we passed the Twin Cities of Minnesota, the landscape shifted from urban to rural.

When we reached the Badlands in South Dakota, my heart cracked open. I had never been west of Chicago prior to this move. Growing up in New York, one feels the city is the center of the universe and that everything important and worthwhile occurs there. But seeing the vistas stretch endlessly before me, I knew there was much more for me to see and learn. I didn't know then that this was Native American land and deeply spiritual to the Lakota Sioux tribe. If I thought we could make a living there, I would have stayed, but instead, we continued on.

In Wyoming, reality set in.

"Karen, watch it!" Mark shouted. I'd been daydreaming. "There's something in the road up ahead."

I braked, slowing to a crawl. We couldn't see clearly what was up ahead, only dark shapes on and around the road. As we approached, we could see cattle scattered over the two-lane highway. Some grazed on the grass lining the side of the road. Some ambled slowly up the highway. Others crossed it. Half a dozen *real* cowboys herded the cattle. The Volvo was stuck in yet another traffic jam, even though there wasn't another car in sight. Mark and I gaped, hoping we wouldn't have to learn to ride horses when we got to Portland.

There was plenty of time during this journey to reflect on my life, but I couldn't let go of the last thing my son had said to me. What kind of woman *would* leave her child? I knew what kind of woman I thought I was, and my thoughts about her were not kind. I had not yet learned to forgive myself and was still a long way from loving myself.

Chapter 9

"You're not done yet!"

<u>Portland, Oregon 1984</u>

We drove in from the North through Vancouver, Washington and across the 205 Bridge. On one side, the Willamette River winds its way through surrounding hillsides dotted with homes. On the other side, the mighty Columbia River graces the city. At one point it forms the Columbia Gorge, famous for windsurfing and cascading waterfalls. During the months of May through October (when the sun actually shines sometimes), Mount Hood majestically towers behind the city's skyline. After a brief stint in a sterile apartment in a not so nice part of town, we found a two-bedroom apartment in an old brick building with high ceilings, wood floors, and a bay window in the living room with a view of Mt. Hood peeking through the trees.

By the time we decided to move to Portland, Mark no longer wanted to be business partners—he wanted to write. Unclear what I wanted and needed for myself, I agreed to support him. I had two choices: find a job or pursue public relations consulting. I sought both options, hoping Spirit would guide me.

After trying out and quitting the most dysfunctional workplace environment I had yet encountered a meeting with a surgery center turned into a consulting gig. When several physicians who practiced at the center wanted to hire me as well, Mark agreed to work together once again.

Over the next two years the business grew, eventually earning almost two hundred and fifty thousand dollars a year. I functioned as co-owner, which included acquiring new business, supervising employees, managing finances, maintaining client relations, and more. Starting a business is thrilling, scary, hectic, and turbulent. In New York, we'd learned the fundamentals of what worked and what didn't. But now we were in a new location. We had to solicit clients, research the media outlets in Oregon, and get a feel for how business was done in a somewhat rural state as opposed to a large urban environment like New York. With each step of growth, I needed to learn new skills and different ways of operating, such as how to hire and fire employees and how to work with the media. Mark still believed the business was his. But when asked what I did, I loved saying I owned a public relations firm and enjoyed the freedom and flexibility that came with owning my own business. We had more money than ever, dependable, hard-working people under us, and an excellent relationship with satisfied clients. David was in my thoughts, but not the focus of my energy and attention, as he'd been when I was in New York. In Portland, I had moments, hours even, when I didn't shrink inside myself with shame for being a mother without her child.

The move from East to West Coast was transformative on several levels. We started attending our twelve-step program meetings immediately, giving us an instant "community" and a forum for my healing to continue. Soon I was able to sort out parental messages and distinguish them from my beliefs and attitudes about money. For one thing, it was okay for me to be happy without feeling selfish. A therapist at the time gave me a wonderful example of what happens when one person in a dysfunctional family begins to heal. Imagine a bucket full of crabs. One crab begins to climb up out of the bucket while the other crabs do all they can to drag that crab back down.

The therapeutic work I'd been doing to heal my childhood wounds began to bear fruit. Several insights emerged. I realized my mother did love me in her own way. I understood that the way I decided to adapt to my family was to pretend to be happy all the time so my parents wouldn't get upset. This led to giving people what I thought they wanted, losing myself in the process. Harder to understand were my conflicting feelings about my son; but I realized that having those conflicting feelings didn't mean I didn't love him. Still, doubts persisted as to whether he loved me.

I wasn't to learn how love really works until I met my husband, Gary, several years later.

The Oregon years were about running a successful business while continuing to work on my own growth and healing. In the daytime, Mark and I and three employees worked at desks disbursed throughout the dining and living areas and along the long hallway which led from the living room to the bedrooms. Our cat, Tiger, perched on different table tops, depending on his mood. Quite often we'd break in the middle of the day to catch a movie or bring the employees ice cream. At night, friends or fellow twelve-steppers came by for late-night chats.

This time period was a bright light after the darkness of the Larry years. Not only did I gain self-respect after a failed marriage and loss of custody of my only child, I was finally creating a meaningful life for myself. Our home bustled with activities. We threw parties, attended meetings, and I continued individual therapy as well as pursuing other self-help options.

The spiritual basis of the twelve-step programs led me to seek out places to practice spirituality, and I soon found comfort in a New Thought Church which preached that there were many paths to God. This philosophy enabled me to incorporate being Jewish with ideas from Christianity, Hinduism, Buddhism, and other great religions of the world. It meant I didn't have to become something else or find God in the path I was born into—it was okay to find my own way. It was there I first learned about the concept of energy in the Universe that we could connect to—sort of like being on a raft on a raging river. You must steer the raft, but the current drives the raft in different directions, its energy carrying you. It was a time of deep spiritual growth. I discovered Louise Hay and her *You Can Heal Your Life*, Deepak Chopra, Dr. Wayne Dyer, and others in the metaphysical/inspirational healing world, many of whom did workshops at the New Thought church I attended.

The business success, our varied activities, and my ongoing pursuit of self-love and acceptance, made me experience gratitude for perhaps the first time. David and I spoke on the phone once a week and our relationship felt closer for awhile. He was more communicative than when I had lived in New York, and I began to think that perhaps I'd been right after all; removing the "pull" he felt between Larry and me *had* eased the pressure on him. It had certainly eased the pressure on me, although guilt kept a residence in my psyche. When asked why my son lived in New York and I lived in Portland, I explained it the way my therapist explained it to me: "You know how they tell you if you're on a crashing plane, you need to put the oxygen on yourself before you can help your child or anyone else? Moving away from David and New York was my oxygen." But although oxygen may save one's life, it doesn't necessarily mend one's broken spirit.

* * *

1986

I wanted sex. By now I'd been celibate for five years and was working in therapy to find a healthy sexuality. After ten years of engaging in a myriad of therapeutic modalities, I felt healed enough to want a complete relationship with a man. Apprehensive, I prayed for God's will, not mine. One day Eddie, tall with thick dirty blonde hair and sea-green eyes, started to attend my Al-Anon meetings. Eddie was unlike any man I'd been interested in before. Both Larry and Mark were Jewish intellectual-types whereas Eddie drove a pick up truck and worked as an inspector, climbing barges and grain elevators to measure qualities and quantities of various products.

Two months later Mark and I hosted a Halloween party. We were playing twister when Eddie and I became entwined, with me underneath him. I looked up into his eyes and blurted, "Can I flirt with you?"

Leaning down, Eddie brushed his lips lightly against mine. A tingle started at the tips of my toes and traveled up. Body parts frozen for years melted with his smile. At thirty-eight-years-old, I was feeling what I imagine teenagers feel when they first get turned on. In all my sexual explorations as a teen, I'd never felt feelings like this before. Those experiences had been about my doing what the boys wanted and expected, hoping they'd like me. My sexual pleasure had not been considered.

One week later, Eddie and I had our first date. After a movie, we went to Papa Hayden's, and over coffee and dessert, we explained our relationships to each other—Mark was gay and Eddie and his wife were separated. His was a distant marriage which allowed for outside dating. A small voice whispered, *oh oh*. I also worried that dating Eddie would change everything with Mark, yet neither of these things stopped me. My body was alive in ways it never had been and there was no way I was going to cork those feelings.

Two months after the "party kiss," I found myself at Eddie's house after an evening out, in bed together for the first time. I wasn't sure what to do or how to do it and my stomach hurt. A bad heartburn flared up during our encounter, but I didn't say anything. Perhaps it was my intuition talking to me, telling me to stop and slow down. But I did not listen. I still had more lessons to learn.

I spent that night at Eddie's (his wife had recently moved to her own apartment with their son) and when I got home the next morning, Mark sat at his desk, typing furiously. The other employees had not yet arrived.

"Happy now?" Mark asked, his face grim.

"I think so," I said. "What's the matter?"

Mark and I had always talked about one or both of us meeting someone else, so I was shocked when Mark said, "I'm not sure I'm ready for this."

"For what?"

"You with another man," he said. "It's going to interfere with the business. It already has."

Conflicting thoughts tore me up inside. I didn't want to lose the life Mark and I had built together. Despite the lack of a sexual relationship, I was relatively happy, at least happier than I'd been up till then in my life. I had a sense of self for the first time. But my loyalty and sense of responsibility towards Mark kept me from acknowledging that perhaps I needed to be away from him to further my recovery. My fear of being on my own and trusting my own instincts paralyzed me.

With hindsight, I could see that I had needed Mark's help when I left Larry. His support and advice got me through losing custody of David. But now, I was convinced that if I sought a conventional relationship, I would lose everything I had—the business, Mark's support, the way he inspired me to improve myself, his brilliance. So I denied how much I wanted a "normal" relationship. I think there's probably always a payoff for staying in denial. Mine was a false sense of security. Jesus preached that you have to be willing to lose your life in order to have it. I had yet to understand that philosophy. I was too afraid of the unknown.

I'm not proud of how I handled this dilemma. For the first few months, I hid my growing feelings for Eddie from Mark. I'd always shared my innermost thoughts and fears with him, so it was hard keeping this secret. In the past, when Mark had periodically attempted to date, it was awkward. I had to endure his bringing people home and my resulting feelings of jealousy and resentment. And before I'd embraced celibacy, when I had attempted dating early on, I had to deal with my own feelings of inadequacy and fear of men and dating. What I had done was to compartmentalize what I felt for Mark so we could continue our life together. Because I eventually stopped dating and basically buried my own needs, sexual and otherwise, things had worked out all right.

But once Eddie came into the picture, he became a catalyst for changing the dynamics between Mark and me. The balance of power shifted. Soon I could separate what Mark was saying about me and my issues from what I felt about them. Suddenly I was able to notice how, when I questioned Mark's comments, things escalated. So I pretended to see things his way in order to placate. If I agreed with him, peace ensued. If I questioned or disagreed, conflict followed.

As I trusted myself and my feelings more and more, my sense of self grew stronger and I recognized I had been stepped on, put down, manipulated and controlled most of my life. The work I'd done since losing custody of David began to coalesce inside me, creating a self-identity where none had existed before. I now wanted a healthy relationship and could see that the one with Mark was not. Perhaps if he'd been straight, we could have negotiated our way to a healthy balance. But that was not the case. This, coupled with the fact that I was in a mutually respectful and pleasurable sexual relationship for the first time, changed me.

But at the same time, I felt as if I were living one of the soap operas I'd been so obsessed with in Plainview. I was with a gay man who was jealous of my new lover and my lover was still married, trying to decide between his marriage and me. As good as the sex felt with Eddie, something also felt wrong, but I wasn't sure what.

One characteristic children who have not received unconditional love in their family might develop is feeling guilty when they stand up for themselves. Somewhere I read that when we feel guilty, we believe we have done something bad; whereas when we feel shame, we believe we *are* bad. Shame makes us feel something is fundamentally wrong with ourselves. This was definitely true for me. I'd felt both these emotions since I was seven—shame about the sexual abuse; shamed by my father; guilty about my parent's miserable marriage (believing it was my fault); shame about losing custody; guilt and shame about leaving my child; and now guilt because I wanted to be with Eddie and Mark was disturbed by this.

But the negative patterns I'd learned as a child were breaking, and I was beginning to find my own voice. I recognized old patterns as they occurred and could change my behavior accordingly. Rather than respond in unconscious, habitual ways, I learned new ones. I knew Mark would be hurt, but I also knew I needed to do what felt right for me. I now believe that in a healthy relationship, both partners can negotiate needs in ways that are not hurtful. But at the time these events occurred, I didn't have the skills to do that.

* * *

"What the hell is this, Karen?"

I looked at Mark. He was brandishing papers I had left on his desk earlier that morning.

"The report I'm going to send to the surgery center," I said.

"It's a piece of crap. You'll need to rewrite it," he said.

Glancing around the apartment, I noticed that each of our three employees had their heads bent over their desks. Obviously, they'd heard this exchange. How different this man was from the Mark who had comforted and supported me through my divorce. I was mortified in front of our staff.

I began to see Mark in a different light, which was disconcerting, because he had been such a strong emotional support for so long. Uncomfortable as my new perceptions were, however, I did start to trust how I felt around Mark, enabling me to make necessary changes. Although my friendship with him had brought me to a more conscious place, it was no longer acceptable to be judged, criticized, and put down. Fear of the unknown became less scary than staying in a situation which now felt abusive. What I couldn't see at the time was Mark's fear of losing me. I didn't have a clue how important I was in anyone's life, still believing I didn't matter. So I lacked empathy for Mark's feelings and his subsequent behavior.

93

In the meantime, Eddie occupied my heart and mind, morning, noon and night. I could not stop thinking about him when he wasn't there and couldn't keep my hands off him when he was there. Signs were ignored that might have warned me he wasn't someone I should settle down with. He was a recovering alcoholic without a program and had only come to Al-Anon because his dad was still actively drinking. Eddie was unwilling or unable to deal with his own drinking problems. Stuck in a dead-end job he hated, he wasn't doing anything to change that situation. What's more, he had a three-year-old son he didn't want to lose. I loved Eddie's relationship with his son and later, wondered if, maybe, in some unconscious way, I was trying to regain my son through Eddie's struggle for his.

As my feelings for Eddie grew, the relationship with Mark suffered. I wrote Mark a letter explaining how sorry I was. After all we'd been through, the last thing I wanted was to hurt him. If I told myself the truth, that I didn't want to live with Mark anymore, I'd have to hurt him and he didn't deserve that. This is a perfect example of why we perpetuate denial. When we stop denying and tell the truth, we are faced with difficult choices and decisions that sometimes hurt others. I believed I owed Mark a tremendous debt of gratitude. He had turned me on to the world of recovery. The business vision had been his. He was a companion and a friend who supported me during the horrendous divorce/custody battle. Yet, while I acknowledged all the things Mark had done for me, I discounted my own part in our relationship. I was a good friend and companion to Mark as well. He'd had a horrible childhood, was uncomfortable being gay, and was just beginning to come to terms with that. Without me, he might not have been able to make his vision of the business a reality. But unfortunately, Mark was so hurt and, I believe, felt so betrayed by me, he couldn't see straight, let alone acknowledge any of my favorable characteristics.

"You're sabotaging our relationship and everything we worked so hard for," Mark responded after reading my letter.

I thought what mattered was our longtime, devoted friendship. I still wanted for him what he wanted for himself, whether it was to own a multi-million dollar PR firm, or to become a world class poet.

"What's changed is how I support those endeavors," I told him. "Other than needing to live by myself and make my own decisions, nothing else has to change."

But Mark didn't see it that way. Looking back now, it is hard for me to imagine that I had been with him for nine years without acknowledging how unhealthy our relationship was. There are men who need women to look, and be a certain way. And there are insecure women who change themselves to keep the relationship. Having no sense of self at the time I met Mark, I understand now why I turned to him. And I did gain some semblance of self from creating a business together. But because I'd given all my power away throughout our time together, and because I had been unable to speak up when I was hurt, angry, or simply disagreed with Mark, when I finally could do all these things, it was too late. The negative patterns were already built into our communications.

Eddie, on the other hand, because he was good looking and attracted to me, elevated a different kind of self-esteem, enough for me to choose to leave Mark, but still not enough to feel okay about it. And my self awareness wasn't developed enough to pay attention when my inner wisdom recognized yet another emotionally unavailable male. Instead, I listened to the horny "teenager" experiencing her sexuality for the first time.

I remained business partners with Mark for a short while, but it quickly became clear that it wasn't working. He was hyper-critical, emotionally distant and cold; I felt tense, irritable and guilty. Plus, we no longer trusted one another. We agreed to split the clients, equipment and assets, and I formed a partnership with one of our employees, Pam. I moved into a lovely one-bedroom apartment in a quiet complex in Beaverton. A stream ran behind the apartment and quite often, I'd take a blanket, a book and my journal and lie on the grass under the shade of a large oak tree with a family of ducks as my only company. Finally, at almost forty, I was on my own.

* * *

1988

Pam and I found an inexpensive office suite, and with our three initial clients, were up and running. Good friends as well as business partners, Pam became a trusted confidante.

95

"It's weird," I said to her one day. "I'm making decisions about sofas, TV's, and towels based on what I think Eddie will like, rather than what I like. In my mind, I am already married to him."

We had many discussions like this about men and relationships. Pam was in an abusive marriage, so she was careful not to give too much advice, but she did caution me not to make the same mistakes.

Eddie and I spent a lot of time together, much of it focused on his divorce and the difficulties he had with his wife over custody of their child. It naturally brought up memories and issues for me regarding David. Unable to acknowledge the pain of that truth, I channeled that energy into supporting Eddie.

My inner feelings were conflicted. The wise woman in me questioned the depth of Eddie's feelings for me. The little girl was afraid of being hurt and rejected. The teenager wanted sex 24/7. If I had known myself better, I would have seen that Eddie came into my life to heal the sexually wounded part of me. I would have understood that he didn't love me the way I wanted and needed to be loved and wouldn't have expected more from him than he was capable of giving. But fear of being alone blocked my ability to hear my own truth.

During my time with Eddie, I began to realize that Spirit had been good to me, and I questioned where the remaining self-hatred came from. I recognized that shame was at the root of my personality and asked myself what I was so ashamed of. I saw that in addition to the shame from the sexual abuse and the promiscuity which followed, plus the shame about being a mother without her child, I was also ashamed of the times I'd denied what I knew was right. I'd dated Larry while he was still engaged to another woman. And by dating Eddie while he was still married, I had once again violated my own ethical code of appropriate behavior. I know now that when I acknowledge to myself that I've done something I believe wrong, I become my harshest judge—harder on myself than any man in any relationship could ever be. The situation with Eddie was no exception. In my opinion, I was a business success and a personal failure.

* * *

1989

Eddie's divorce became final and he was awarded joint custody of his son. As our relationship moved forward, I became more involved with child care issues and as a result, developed a relationship with Eddie's ex-wife. During one of our many conversations about child drop-off times and places, we discussed Eddie and me, and when we had started dating. She confirmed what Eddie had told me about their relationship at the time he and I had met, releasing me from the shame I had felt for dating a married man. He had, indeed, been free to date others. But she also told me they'd slept together after he and I had become a couple. Eddie had lied to me about that.

Doubts plagued me. I woke up wondering whether Eddie really loved me and went to sleep thinking he cared for me as a friend, not a lover. Over time, the intensity and frequency of our lovemaking lessoned. It was now two years into our relationship and I needed to know how Eddie really felt. Either he was in love with me or he wasn't. If he was, I needed him to show it.

One night, I sat him down in my living room.

"Until now, I understood you were dealing with your divorce and custody issues and I've been patient," I told him. "But I need a commitment. I need to know where I stand with you."

"I'll think about it," Eddie said.

About a month later, despite not feeling loved the way I wanted to be, when Eddie proposed on my fortieth birthday, I accepted. Though I may never know what compelled him to ask, or why I unhesitatingly said yes, the wedding date was set. That June, with Eddie's son and mother, and Pam as witnesses, we were married in the office of two ministers of the New Thought Church we'd been attending.

As during my first marriage, I gained weight immediately, even though prior to our wedding, Eddie had specifically asked me not to. Problems with Eddie's son interfered with our relationship, as did stress over money. I began hypnotherapy to further reveal and heal the issues that still plagued me. This therapy catapulted me into a deeper level of recovery, but grappling with such intense emotions negatively impacted my marriage. Depression once again troubled me, and, as it had before, food consoled me.

I questioned whether the PR business was what I really wanted to do; however, I didn't want to go back to being a secretary. I had worked too hard to become a public relations executive. But it was increasingly difficult to force myself to make cold sales calls. Mark had been the one with the driving ambition, pushing both of us further and harder to succeed. Finding the energy to motivate without him was not easy.

In addition, my guilt over leaving David escalated. He visited once a year, but the visits were stilted. We were strangers who happened to be mother and child. I started to admit that the choices and decisions I had made might not have been the best and continued to blame myself for the resulting problems. And the weight kept piling on.

By marrying Eddie I had deluded myself once again into believing that if he loved me, we would live happily ever after. But life is not a fairy tale, and the deterioration of this marriage was much more painful than my previous one, primarily because I had worked so hard and so long to heal and yet, still had made another poor relationship choice.

1991

Eddie and I went through the motions: we traveled back and forth to work, ate dinner and watched TV. In the beginning, I enjoyed interrupting Eddie's football games by seducing him, but now I didn't try and he rarely initiated.

David grew from age eleven to twenty-one during my Oregon years. We spoke on the phone every few weeks and when David arrived for his yearly visit, we'd make an effort to be a family. But as a seventeen-year-old teenager, how could he relate to a six-year-old stepbrother he only saw once a year? And how was I to connect with this young man I barely knew? It was an unnatural way for a mother and child to relate.

A few months after David's 1991 visit, I was expecting an invitation to attend his high school graduation. But instead, a letter arrived from David informing me that he did not want me to come. When I called to discuss his request, he went even further, telling me he did not want anything to do with me anymore.

Losing David a second time was beyond belief. Only this time I wouldn't get to see or speak to him at all. He wanted no contact. *What did I do to deserve this? I don't blame him. Despite resenting my parents for everything they hadn't given me, I still spoke to them, still visited them. It must be Larry, damn it. He's poisoned David against me. No, I did that myself by leaving New York.*

My monkey mind was a continuous screech. Eddie was useless in situations like this, and I no longer had Mark to talk to. Pam was some help, but we were in the midst of deciding whether to keep our business together, so our relationship was complicated. I did the only thing I knew to rid myself of the pain in my gut. I ate and slept, ate and slept, ate and slept, slipping into my comfort zone; an inner place I entered which created a barrier that pain couldn't penetrate. Once the pain was numbed, I could think things through. I wrote David the following letter.

6/18/91

Dear David:

For many years, I was angry at my parents because they didn't take care of my needs when I was growing up, so I understand and don't blame you for how you are feeling.

It took me years to process what happened to me growing up. It's too easy to judge others, especially when we only have one side of a story, or only consider our own feelings and perceptions. There are things about my life with your father, my childhood, the divorce, that you do not know which caused me to make the decisions I made. I know that doesn't make you feel better or ease your pain or lessen the anger. And I'm not trying to make excuses for my behavior. I so wish I could go back and do some things differently. But we can't change the past. We have only today and all the tomorrows.

I finally realized that my parents did the best they could with the skills they had (which were few). It doesn't make my childhood better, but I no longer judge them and am no longer angry with them. I hope some day you will come to feel that way about me. I truly did the best I could with the knowledge I had at the time, which, unfortunately for both of us, wasn't very much. I wish you didn't feel the need to break away from me so completely, but I guess I will have to learn to live with it. Please know I wish you much love, joy, peace and success in your life. My heart, my love, and my life will be open to you when, and if, you choose to come back.

God Bless you.
Mom

* * *

It would be four years before I spoke with my son again—four years of soul-searching which alternated between being unable to understand David's decision and agreeing with it completely. *Why should he want me in his life? I don't deserve him.* I survived and functioned by eating to numb the pain. Life had to go on. On the weekends Eddie's son was with us, I made him breakfast and lunch, and took him out to play. I also worked a business I was good at, but which no longer satisfied me.

As the shock of David's decision wore off, the hollowness inside became a constant. Raw and vulnerable, Eddie and I climbed into bed one night and I turned to face him, body pressed against body. Reaching up, I stroked Eddie's thick hair, letting my hand trail down his back. But Eddie's lips remained passive, and when I leaned in to kiss him, his arms stayed at his sides rather than wrapping around me the way they used to. I pulled back and Eddie quickly rolled over, his back to me—my one hundred ninety-four-pound body creating quite a distance between us. Part of me didn't blame Eddie for not wanting me sexually at that time. But part of me craved a man who wanted me no matter how I looked—a man who loved the me that is me—not the externals. I'm lucky enough to have that now in my marriage to Gary, but at the time, neither Eddie nor I knew that underneath the flesh I'd covered myself in were deep pockets of shame and hurt I still hadn't learned to release.

In the meantime, I supported our household while Eddie figured out his next career move. It had been my idea for him to quit his job; however, I had no idea he would be so slow to choose his next step. Eddie and I were in therapy with his ex-wife to help their son. I was in therapy to resolve my issues. Eddie and I were in couples' therapy. And things still sped rapidly downhill.

Not being able to parent my son made me feel like a leper. Sure, I believed I had good reasons for the choices I had made. But the bottom line was, when I'd left New York, I'd removed any chance of having input in David's life. I'd left because I couldn't parent him the way I'd wanted and I couldn't figure out how to bridge the emotional barrier between us. And I'd needed to heal my own self. But David didn't know that, and now he'd rejected me.

He continued to communicate with and visit my parents, so through them, I kept up with his activities. He went to a private college on Long Island; part of that time spent abroad. When I heard these things from my mom, I'd sob so hard, I'd have to rush off the phone.

My depression manifested itself with total lethargy. Tired and drained, I could not make myself do much beyond basic household chores. This time, in addition to having no energy, I was irritable, with severe mood swings. At their worst, I saw no reason to keep living. Several years later I was diagnosed with peri-menopause. But even if hormones played a part in the negative way I felt, at the core was my belief that I was a complete and utter failure. Then a movement technique called Non-Impact Aerobics (NIA) entered my life and my spirit slowly began to mend.

* * *

The Dance, 1991

Pam and I mutually agreed to dissolve our business, and I accepted a position as PR director with an ad agency. Their major client was a health care firm called Qual-Med and it was my primary account responsibility. Qual-Med's marketing director was a woman named Betsy, who became a dear friend until she died in 2004.

In 1991, I quit that agency to help start a non-profit organization called Healthy Start, which provided pre-natal care to low income women. It paid less than I had been earning when Eddie and I met. Miserable in my marriage and lacking the money I had grown accustomed to, suicidal thoughts once again rose to the surface.

Through this rough period, however, I became friends with the Administrative Assistant at Healthy Start. Lyssa was an unusual woman with dark auburn hair and green eyes who went barefoot everywhere. At our office, she'd light incense when no one else was around—her exotic looks and strange ways made coworkers keep their distance, but I was fascinated by her and her story.

A former professional dancer, Lyssa helped me get a handle on my physical health during a short period in which she lived with Eddie and me. It was she who introduced me to NIA, a series of dance moves choreographed to music. NIA really connected to the dancer in me—the dancer I had shut down at seven when I quit dancing school. After attending classes for about six months, I decided to take an intensive workshop offered by the founders of the program.

"Each of you will dance for ten minutes alone, just you and the music," Carlos said. Eight of us were seated cross-legged on the floor in the dance studio. We were strangers, participants in this weeklong training to become White Belt NIA Dance Instructors. Unlike the other trainees, I was there to improve my self-esteem while trying to figure out my next career strategy. It had been thirty-five years since I'd last danced in public.

"Do we get to choose our own music?" I asked.

Carlos shook his head no, his long black ponytail swaying across his muscular back. As one of the two founders of NIA, he ran the "free dance" portion of the training. We learned not to question him. He had his reasons for doing things a certain way— dark, mysterious reasons from his Cuban heritage that we white women didn't understand. Debbie, his partner, sat quietly next to the stereo, ready to play the pieces Carlos had chosen for each student.

"You will go in this order," Carlos said, calling out each of our names.

"Great," I whispered to Marti, seated next to me in the small studio of our instructors' basement. "I get to have a panic attack waiting for my turn."

"You'll be fine," she said. "Everything we've learned has led up to this moment. Don't worry, Worry Wart."

"That's fine for you to say," I replied. "You are a perfect size six. I'm a perfect hippo."

Carlos signaled Debbie to start the music and Suzanne stood up. Tall, sinewy, blonde, wearing a pink leotard and opaque tights, Suzanne walked to the center of our circle, closed her eyes for a moment, took a deep breath and began to move. I watched her for a few seconds, envying her body, her height, her hair, but I especially envied her freedom of movement. Closing my eyes, I willed the knot in my gut away.

A few minutes later, I opened them. To my surprise, three dancers had already finished. Just two remained before it was my turn. The knot grew into a burn that traveled to my chest, then spread to my throat and I gagged.

"I don't think I can do this," I said to Marti.

"It's your choice, Karen. But remember what Carlos said: 'If we don't face our fears, they'll continue to haunt us.' She was right. This was why I had signed up for the workshop in the first place. But how could I get up in front of these people weighing one hundred ninety-four pounds, a good seventy pounds heavier than the others, and pretend I was one of them?

Carlos turned to me, his dark eyes smiling. "Okay, Karen, it's your turn."

I put my hands flat on the floor and pushed my body up, so out of shape I needed to hold onto the mirrored wall for support. I was not a person who perspired much, but sweat ran down the back of my neck and between my breasts, a dark spot forming on my light blue leotard. I walked slowly to the center of the circle, feeling the heat in the small room, inhaling its musky odor. Out of the corner of my eye, I saw Carlos give Debbie the signal to start the music. I prayed for some connection to it.

"Remember to breathe, Karen," Carlos said, smiling up at me from his seat in the corner.

The music began, sounding like it was far off in a tunnel. The recessed lights in the ceiling seemed overly bright. Ten pairs of eyes focused entirely on my fat body; I was the center of everyone's attention, and I froze. Closing my eyes to shut everything out, I saw myself at seven years old, holding out the ends of my pink tutu as I twirled in front of the mirror—before my father came backstage and called me a whore. The part of me who wanted to be a dancer and had given up that dream rose to the surface. I opened my eyes and listened. The music wasn't familiar to me, but my heart beat in rhythm with the drums. Slowly my body began to sway to the tune of the string instruments. After several minutes, I danced as if I were that innocent girl alone in her room, before the painter molested me or the nightmare of the dance recital shut me down. I felt connected to everything and all was connected to me. For those precious moments I was fully present and awake, my body moving freely and easily. Allowing the music to take me where it wanted me to go, my arms swayed like the branches of a willow tree; my body twisted like a Cobra snaking up out of a basket. When my ten minutes were over, the music ended. Something long buried had surfaced.

* * *

103

Over the next few years, I continued to take NIA classes with Debbie and Carlos and lost about twenty pounds. Lyssa had become part of my family. She started calling me "sister" and Eddie "brother." Lyssa had no living relatives, so we included her in our family birthday celebrations, Thanksgiving dinners, and other special occasions. When things with Eddie and I unraveled to a degree that felt unmanageable, I stayed at Lyssa's place on the weekends Eddie had custody of his son. Peace entered my soul there.

"Come on, Karen, upsy daisy," Lyssa said as she hauled me off the couch. "Help me with the stir fry."

Another night she encouraged me with, "Let's take Blackie for a walk." Blackie was a pitch black dog Lyssa had found while running in the park one day. Blackie, along with Lyssa's sassy Siamese cat, became part of my new "weekend family."

With some distance from Eddie and his son, I began to sort through my feelings. This was all too familiar territory—being married to someone who didn't seem to love and appreciate me for who I was, although Eddie had seemed to feel that way in the beginning. I supposed my increasing depression and my ever-expanding body contributed to Eddie's withdrawal. Leaving his job probably also had something to do with it. And the ongoing issues with his son exacerbated already difficult communication styles and modes of behavior between us. I made one last attempt to work things out with Eddie by choosing to eliminate my weekend stays at Lyssa's. I couldn't run away. If we were going to make it, we had to live together as a family.

"Karen, leave him alone," Eddie said one night, several weeks later.

Eddie's son stood in the doorway of his room complaining of a stomachache. I told him to get back into bed. Every night it was a different excuse. Sometimes he was thirsty, sometimes hungry. This night it was his stomach hurting. His therapist and I knew the child was trying to manipulate us in order to stay up later, but Eddie wasn't buying. Later, after his son finally went to sleep, Eddie said he didn't believe I loved the boy. I threw up my hands. We were at a stalemate. How could I stay with someone who didn't believe I was a loving person? Why would I want to? Still, I wasn't ready to give up.

What did become clear was that I couldn't handle any more negativity from Eddie about my behavior. The progress I had made in developing a self-identity was eroding, and I was not willing to let it totally vanish. I had the best of intentions for those I loved, but I also had the best of intentions for myself, and what was happening was unacceptable. My limit had been reached. This was obviously a sensitive area for me. With the divorce from Larry came the loss of Carol, Margaret, Grammy and Poppy. When I started the business with Mark and began to focus on myself, I'd lost custody of David. And when I'd moved from New York, I'd eventually lost David altogether. When I found Eddie, I'd lost Mark. Now I was concerned about the impact another divorce would have on Eddie's son and terrified I would lose yet another family.

* * *

October 1993

"Eddie, I need more time together," I said. We'd been married almost four years and together for six. "We never make time to talk, go to a movie, or make love anymore."

With his eyes still glued to the football game, Eddie shrugged his shoulders. "What do you want from me? Nothing would be enough for you, Karen."

"How about ten minutes in the morning, before we leave for work? It could be our cuddle time, a place to wish each other a good day. Then ten minutes at night, when we get home to re-connect; see how each other's day went."

Eddie thought for a minute. "You'd never be satisfied with ten minutes in the morning and ten minutes at night," he said as he turned back to the game.

Lyssa felt differently than I did and I wondered if she saw things in Eddie I didn't. Pictures of her and Eddie together flashed in my mind's eye. They seemed so much better suited. It occurred to me that Lyssa and I could simply change places.

A short time later, I found a book I thought would help us resolve some of our issues called *Men Are from Mars; Women Are from Venus*, by John Gray. In the book, Gray talks about the fact that men mistakenly expect women to think and communicate the way men do, and women mistakenly expect men to feel and communicate the way women do. Gray said we forget men and women are supposed to be different and, as a result, our relationships are filled with unnecessary friction and conflict. As I read on, I saw Eddie and me all over the pages and became convinced this book could help us. Perhaps if we understood the different ways we perceived and processed issues, the marriage *could* succeed.

Eddie agreed to read the book and we made an appointment to talk two weeks later. A spark of hope ignited. I was sure the explanations Gray gave in his book would help our marriage. For example, Gray explains, "To feel better, Martians go to their caves to solve problems alone. To feel better, Venusians get together and openly talk about their problems." This, as well as other examples Gray provided, showed me how Eddie and I could change the dynamics that were destroying our marriage.

The night of our "date" arrived. Eddie's son was at his mom's. I made Eddie's favorite dinner, chili and corn bread, and even waited awhile for him to wind down (One of his complaints had been that I assaulted him the minute he walked in the door, demanding attention). At my insistence, he'd gotten a part-time job as a bank teller so he could make his monthly child support payments.

About an hour later, I asked, "So, what did you think of the book? Isn't it interesting?"

"What book?" he asked. "What are you talking about?"

Our marriage ended for me in that moment. If I wasn't important enough for him to remember what he had agreed to do, then I would never truly feel loved. I wanted more than crumbs and had finally reached a place where I felt I deserved better. And if he didn't really love me, he deserved more as well.

I moved in with Lyssa full-time. It was supposed to be a trial separation, and I only planned to stay with her until I found a job, but that is not how it turned out. I had quit the non-profit organization to train to be a hypnotherapist, but wasn't committed yet. Even though hypnotherapy had proven to be a powerful therapeutic tool for me, I wasn't sure someone without proper mental health credentials should practice it.

My life was a black hole. I had no contact with my son. I wasn't sure what I wanted to explore next in terms of work. Worry about Eddie's son kept me up at night. Even though I was exercising, I was still heavy and hated how I looked. I was practically broke and had major concerns around Lyssa being so "giving" to Eddie and his family, afraid I'd lose them all.

One day I asked her, "Can't you put a hold on your relationship with Eddie while I'm living with you?"

"I don't see why I should," she said, tossing her long hair.

Baffled and feeling betrayed, I watched as Lyssa took my place in Eddie's family, just as I had envisioned, feeling much the same way I had when I lost Carol because of divorcing Larry. I didn't blame Eddie and Lyssa for falling for each other; my relationship with Eddie had already died by the time Lyssa came into the picture. But regardless of the reasons, I was being left yet again.

"Where are you going?" I asked her one day, several months after Eddie informed me he wanted a divorce.

"We're going to celebrate Mom and Dad's anniversary," she said.

Mom and Dad were Eddie's parents and I, of course, was not invited. Sitting on the edge of Lyssa's bed, I watched her put make-up on and comb her long hair. She gave me a quick hug before running barefoot out the door, Blackie at her heels.

Betsy, the marketing manager I'd befriended at Qual-Med, came over and held me as I sobbed.

"Karen, honey, you must realize she and Eddie are in a relationship—and not a brother and sister one," Betsy said gently.

Weeks earlier, I'd asked Lyssa about her sexual relationship with Eddie, but she had denied it repeatedly. How someone could be such a good friend in so many ways but lie to me and betray me in others was beyond my comprehension. I was living with a woman I had become close to, trying to understand why yet another marriage had ended, and watching her grow closer and closer to the family I had lost. At this point Eddie had stopped communicating with me, so I lost him, his son, and his mom. It was the third time I lost a family and group of friends (Larry, Mark, and now Eddie) and my chest felt so burdened with the weight of the pain, I honestly didn't think I could survive it and I wasn't sure I even wanted to.

"Are you going to NIA tonight?" I asked Lyssa when she got home from work a few days later.

"No, I'm playing tennis with a friend," she said as she grabbed her racket and walked back out of the apartment. Watching from the window as she got into her car, I saw Eddie sitting in the passenger seat. Deep sobs wracked my body as I lay on the sofa in fetal position. Hours passed and darkness swept into the living room. I sat, lights off, chest heaving, wishing there was a bottle of sleeping pills in the medicine cabinet. Instead, I called my friend Suzi and made an appointment for a hypnotherapy session the next day.

After our session, I told Suzi I had an urge to go to the Southwest. Debbie and Carlos (my NIA instructors) had recently returned from Santa Fe raving about how spiritual a place New Mexico was. "There's a shaman on every corner," Debbie had said.

"Why don't you go?" Suzi asked.

"I have no money," I said.

"Perhaps there's a way," Suzi responded.

A few days later, I told Lyssa, "I can't stay here and watch you and Eddie run off together. I'm going to leave Portland and explore the Southwest."

"I'm sorry things turned out this way," Lyssa said.

"Me too," I said, not believing she was sorry at all.

At a garage sale, I sold everything I could. The plan was to leave Oregon in order to recover from this latest loss and heal once again. Two weeks later, I was on my way. Somewhere in the middle of the Mojave Desert, I wrote Lyssa a letter telling her I could no longer remain friends with someone who treated me so callously. We never spoke again.

* * *

May 1994

I left the Pacific Northwest with clothes, TV, and computer packed in my Toyota, not knowing for sure where I would land or how I would live. The twenty-seven hundred dollars I had made in the garage sale was now all the money I had in the world. It was one of those dark-nights-of-the-soul times in my life when I felt completely empty after yet another failed relationship.

I'd lost just about everything and everyone important in my life—my son, families, old friends, my business—and most assuredly the self I had worked so hard to find. The trip was planned so I could stay with people I knew in Oregon the first few days, stay with another friend in

San Francisco after that, then go to Pam, who had moved to Los Angeles. Once I left L.A., I would be on my own.

The day I left on my journey, high, gray and white clouds filled the Oregon sky. I checked and double checked the contents of the car, smiling as I poked through the trunk and saw the care package my friend Dennis had provided. Ever practical, he'd given me emergency provisions in case the car died—flares, a flashlight, that kind of thing. My photo albums were packed in one box, my journals in two others.

My stomach fluttered, but it wasn't the whirling dervish kind of feeling that signaled acute anxiety. This felt more like butterflies when I'm happy about something. I got in the car, said a prayer, and took off. I'd only been driving a few miles when I looked up and noticed a group of hawks soaring above my car, a sign that I was being guided. During one of my hypnotherapy sessions, I had been working on integrating the needy child inside with the wise adult woman. The therapist asked how I could differentiate between the desires of a child that might be harmful and the normal wishes a child has. An eight-foot hawk with a twenty-foot wing span sped into my vision and swept the small child (me) onto its back. Its piercing eyes stayed focused ahead and the child that was me felt secure. The hawk re-appeared in subsequent sessions, and I came to understand that it represented my intuition. Whenever I was in doubt, that same hawk would come show me the way. It became a powerful symbol of wisdom and strength. So as I began this solo journey, seeing the hawks assured me I was doing the right thing. I felt lucky as those magnificent raptors followed me for the first few miles.

My first stop was in southern Oregon in a town called Ashland. There I stayed with two friends whom I'd met in hypnotherapy training.

"Where are you heading?" Kate asked.

"I'm not sure," I said. "I feel drawn to Arizona and New Mexico."

Kate offered to call her parents, who lived in Albuquerque. When she came back into the room, she said her mother's friend, Mary Alice, was looking for a house-sitter in three weeks. I agreed to do it. That date gave me plenty of time to stop at Big Sur, the Grand Canyon, and Sedona along the way, places I'd always wanted to see.

But while driving through the Mojave Desert, doubts gnawed at my insides. Friends in Portland had thrown a good-bye party before I left, and the loving wishes and excitement of adventure had carried me this far. Now, however, the starkness of the landscape, which stretched for miles on either side of the highway, filled me with a deep sense of emptiness. There were few vehicles on the road and the intense heat of the day permeated the car so that even the air-conditioning couldn't keep me cool. Gripping the steering wheel hard, I kept my eyes focused on the white line dividing the highway, but soon tears blinded me. *I can't do this anymore. I have failed at everything. It doesn't matter. I don't matter to anyone. I'm not sure I ever did.* I wanted to die. At the next rest stop, I pulled over and thought about leaving the windows up, motor turned off. *With this heat, it won't take long.* But a voice whispered inside my head. *You're not done here yet, Karen. You're going to be okay. Just keep going.*

"I don't want to!" I screamed back. "I'm so tired. I can't do it anymore."

Yes, you can, the voice whispered. *You are not alone.*

There is no way to know how long I sat there sobbing. At some point, I reached behind me to grab a scrapbook my friends had given me. It was filled with wishes for well being and happiness on my journey as well as poems and prayers letting me know how courageous they thought I was for undertaking such an adventure. Pretty soon I had to pee. The rest stop was completely deserted. It was late afternoon and I needed a place to stay. I had plenty of food in the cooler in my backseat, but I didn't want to be looking for a motel in a strange town after dark.

I used the facility, climbed back into the car, and picked up the scrapbook once again. "You are so brave," Betsy had written. "I'm jealous," her husband Bob had scrawled. "Let the open road take you to your next step," Carlos had said. "You are a Spiritual Seeker. You will find your way."

Brave? I'm homeless. But I kept reading and the love emanating from their words slipped into my consciousness. In the moments that followed, I understood in every fiber of my being that I wasn't alone and never had been. Guidance had been there all along. I just hadn't learned to listen.

* * *

When my house-sitting stint was over, Mary Alice offered to let me stay with her while I figured out if I wanted to make my new home in Albuquerque. She was seventy-two and widowed. She'd moved to

Albuquerque from Pasadena just two years before my arrival. She is petite, about 5'2", with gray hair worn in a short pageboy cut. Her blue eyes sparkle when she speaks. As a former schoolteacher, she is articulate and well informed about world events. The only money she would accept from me was for food and phone calls. From my lovely room overlooking the city, I would lie on my bed each evening and watch the sun set. On the other side of the house, the moon rose behind the Sandia Mountains. Soon I understand why New Mexico is called The Land of Enchantment.

* * *

One day Mary Alice took me to the Indian Pueblo Cultural Center where she serves as a docent. As we walked through the museum, a fellow traveler joined us, wanting to hear Mary Alice's explanation of the nineteen pueblos and their history. She invited the man, whose name was Earl, back to her home that night for dinner. Earl was a handyman and over the next few days, camped in Mary Alice's back yard so he could fix her picnic table, among other things. Earl invited me to go camping the following weekend at Chaco Canyon, a sacred place to the Pueblo tribes located on the eastern edge of Arizona, just north of Window Rock.

As Earl was an experienced camper, it didn't take long to set up camp. We pitched our tent at the base of a large mesa and that night went to sleep with the hoot of the owls and the howls of the coyotes the only sounds to pierce the deep silence. The night sky sparkled with more stars than I'd ever seen in my life.

The following morning, we went our separate ways, Earl to hike the ridge of the rocks while I explored the Anasazi ruins of Pueblo Bonito. In recent years, the Kiva, the ceremonial space the Anasazi used for ritual, became off limits to visitors. But that day I was able to walk down into it. Sitting on the ledge which surrounded the circular stone wall inside the Kiva with legs tucked up and my chin resting on my knees, I allowed the silence to soothe my soul. I thought I was imagining things when I heard the ancient spirits of the Anazasi whisper in nonverbal language, but came away with a sense that I was where I needed to be for the next stage of my growth. My journal was with me and as I listened to the unintelligible whispers and felt peace wrap its arms around me, I

111

reflected on my life. After three hours spent alone in the Kiva, these words gradually emerged:

I stand on the outside of the circle, alone and afraid.
All my life I've felt outside of things, disconnected.
Outside of my parents, outside of my marriages, outside of my child, outside of my careers.
I stopped hearing my own voice, my own song.
I stopped listening to the whispers of my heart's desire, my intuition, my deep, inner longings.
I danced your dance. Heard your song. Listened to the whispers of your wishes and dreams.

Spirit has spoken to me, in the long dark night of my soul's searching.
My song is calling to me. It is time to listen.
My life is my free dance. The people, the events, my thoughts and my feelings, the music that moves me.
All around the circle, the events of my life ebb and flow and I dance to the tune of each.
Until now I danced your tune, listened to your thoughts, participated in your events.

I am on the inside of the circle now.
Spirit teaches, guides, and protects me.
I must be quiet so I can hear my song.
I release my fear. Spirit moves through me.
My body sways to the rhythm of my dreams.
Alone in the midst of the circle of my life, I finally learn to dance my own dance.

This was a powerful moment—the culmination of my searching for Self and finding comfort with aloneness and solitude. I'd finally come to terms with my fear of being alone and how that had kept me choosing inappropriate partners and staying with them long after I knew the relationship wouldn't work.

112

Chapter 10

Coming Home

Shortly after accepting Mary Alice's generous offer, I called the Albuquerque division of Qual-Med and reached a woman named Grace. She provided communication services in New Mexico, the same work I had done for the Portland branch in my capacity as PR director at the ad agency. Betsy, as Qual-Med's marketing director, had been reluctant to see me leave the city, but as my friend, she'd cheered me on. Betsy had suggested Qual-Med would be a great place to network in what might be my new home state. When Grace walked into the restaurant, however, I wanted to grab my portfolio and run as fast as I could out the back door.

Grace looked the way I wanted to. She is about 5'7", thin with wavy brown hair. Her make-up was subtle, and she wore feminine clothing in earth tones that enhanced her olive skin. Her sultriness made me feel dowdy. But my desire to find work overpowered my instinct to run. When Grace sat down opposite me her smile did not reach her lovely green eyes. Early on in life I'd learned to recognize someone else's pain.

"So what brought you to Albuquerque?" Grace asked after we ordered lunch.

"My husband fell in love with my best friend," I said, watching her eyes cloud over. "Our marriage was already in trouble, though, so I can't

113

really blame her."

Grace toyed with the salad on her plate. About to jump into the silence with even more private information, I hesitated a moment, choosing to eat my French fries instead.

"I'm getting a divorce as well," said Grace. "My husband asked me to move out of the house. I'm staying with a friend while he draws up the papers; he's a very successful attorney here in town. He didn't even pretend to want to work things out. One day it was over, just like that."

Reaching across the table, I held Grace's hand, and when we stood up to say goodbye a short while later, we hugged like old friends.

"I'll get those names and numbers to you by the end of the week," Grace said as she turned to go. She walked down the aisle on high heels that would have made me topple. A few weeks later we met again, this time on a Friday. I asked Grace what she was doing that night.

"Folk dancing," she said. "Why don't you come?"

There were about seventy people dancing outside on the plaza in front of Zimmerman Library on the University of New Mexico campus. Many of the dances were line or circle, so no partner was required. But every other dance was for couples and once again I was back in Junior High School when no one asked me out. After an hour I told Grace I had to leave. She mentioned another group which met on a different night, one with older people where I might feel more comfortable. When I tried that group the following week, I found Grace had been right and began to attend it regularly.

Most of the dancers in the second folkdance group were in their sixties and seventies, so I was quite surprised when an adorable man, younger than the others, walked in one night. He was short and wiry, with salt and pepper hair and beard and twinkling turquoise eyes. He appeared to be with a woman, though, so I didn't pay much attention. Later in the evening, the woman introduced me to the man, whose name was Gary. She was visiting from Atlanta and explained that she and Gary were not a couple, just dancing buddies. That night Gary didn't say anything to me except hello and for the next few weeks we didn't speak to each other at all.

* * *

114

My time with Mary Alice helped me come to terms with how I felt being single again at forty-six. She led an active life and seemed content, despite having no male partner. She was the first happy single woman I'd ever known, helping me see that perhaps I didn't need a partner either—that one could be happy *and* alone. I think those who have the opportunity to go off to college, away from the home they grew up in, learn this lesson at that time. But I never had that chance. This was my time to stand on my own two feet, attempting to discover who I was, not in relation to a man or a child or a parent.

One week led to the next and some public relations consulting came my way, but I found no permanent job prospects. Four months passed and my savings were nearly gone. As a fallback, I planned to stay with my parents in Florida to figure out what next, but just before I was ready to leave, a job as PR director for an ad agency came my way. Within a few short weeks, I found an apartment, bought some furniture, and began to build a life in New Mexico. Just as the idea of being content and single was settling into my psyche, the phone rang one night. I'd just finished preparing my dinner.

"I hate to be the one to tell you, but Eddie and Lyssa have moved in together," Betsy said. She and I had remained friends and over the last few months I'd heard bits and pieces she had shared about Eddie and Lyssa. Although I had known this might come, it still felt like a kick in the gut. I'd been attending the folkdance group for about three months when this phone call came and hoped dancing might help me forget this heartache. When Betsy and I hung up, I finished eating, did the dishes, and left to go dancing.

For awhile, the music and the movement helped me forget the news I'd just received. During a break in the music program, I went to the kitchen for a drink of water.

"Hey, Karen," said one of the male participants. "I haven't had much of a chance to talk to you. What brought you to Albuquerque?" He was married, so I knew he wasn't hitting on me.

I burst out crying. Gary walked by and gently wiped my tears, not saying a word. The rest of that evening, Gary stood next to me and goofed around, trying to get me to laugh. Touched by his behavior and wanting to thank him, I asked him to go for coffee or dinner.

Gary suggested the Macaroni Grill and we met there the following week. During dinner, the chatter of other patrons, the clattering of dishes and the loud opera singing at the next table compensated for the lack of conversation at ours. Gary did say he had noticed me dancing and wanted to ask me out, but couldn't summon the courage, so he was glad I had invited him. That was pretty much all Gary said that evening, and I began to think we didn't have much in common. Just when I had pretty much decided that I wouldn't go out with him again, a voice inside my head whispered, *Give this one a chance*. It was the same voice that had questioned what I was doing on the morning of my wedding to Larry; the same voice that had advised me to get out of EST; the same one that had expressed doubts about Eddie. And the same one that had whispered to me in the Mojave Desert that I wasn't alone—I wasn't finished yet.

When dinner was over, Gary walked me to my car. As I opened the door and turned to say goodnight, Gary wrapped his arms around me and leaned in for a kiss. His lips were soft and warm and his moustache felt rough, but the kiss delighted me. I didn't expect such a shy man to be so bold on a first date.

When Gary called a few days later asking if I wanted to hike the following weekend, I almost said no, but chose instead to listen to what I now believe to be the voice of Spirit.

My one and only hike had been when a friend took me to Mt. Hood in Oregon. I'd fallen several times and sprained my ankle, so I did not think I was cut out for hiking.

"Okay, but not a real long hike," I said, nervous Gary would discover how un-athletic and out of shape I was.

We drove to Jemez Springs in Gary's Ford Explorer, his dog Wolfie in the backseat. This time Gary was a bit more talkative, telling me about growing up one of five children in a small, West Texas town.

"Are you divorced?" I asked.

"No," he said. "I've never been married."

"How old are you?"

"Forty-three."

Uh oh. Forty-three and never been married. Is he a closet gay? What's wrong with him that he never married?

"I'm forty-six and I've been married twice," I said. "And I was partners with a gay man," I added, thinking if I told him everything right up front and it didn't scare him away, we'd be ahead of the game. I did not,

116

however, tell him that day how deeply ashamed I was for my marital failures. Gary quietly held my hand as we walked through the old train tunnel that leads to the waterfall cascading down the canyon walls. There were no questions, no raised eyebrows, no frowns, or pulling away as I shared my story—just a warm glow emanating from his clear eyes. My heart did not beat wildly as it had when I met Eddie. But it felt tender and safe when Gary touched me.

After several dates, I invited Gary to my apartment for pizza and a movie. After eating, we started to watch the movie and before I knew it, we were kissing on the couch.

"I'm scared," I said. "My experiences with sex are not that positive."

"Me either," Gary said. "But you are so beautiful and it feels right, doesn't it?"

"I think so."

I was terrified of making another mistake. But there was a difference with Gary—I felt good with him right away. Gary would listen to me, hear how I felt, and not put me down or ridicule me. But since Eddie had been attracted to me when I was thin and stopped wanting to make love when I'd gained weight, I had a hard time believing Gary wanted me, since my weight was up again—one hundred eighty-three pounds.

Although I was uncomfortable with my sexuality, I *was* comfortable with Gary, so the sex that night was gentle and sweet. But I was wary, not trusting me or him or relationships. I decided to test him. Over the next few months, every sordid detail of my past made it into our conversations. When my parents visited, I introduced them, convinced that would make him shy away from me. I shared that I wanted to quit my job. No matter what I said, or how shocking or revealing, Gary still treated me with respect and continued to show interest in being with me.

I'd had an image of what I thought I needed in a relationship and had tried to mold my partners to fit that picture. With Gary, I let the image go (it hadn't worked anyway). This was new relationship territory. I didn't "need" anything from Gary, nor he from me. And for the first time, there were no warning signs that he was interested in someone else or wasn't as interested in me as I was in him. None of the issues which had been present in previous relationships were evident. My priorities were straight about what was important to me. With Eddie, it was sex

117

that I needed. With Mark, it was psychological and emotional advice and support. With Larry, it was having a husband and family of my own. I'd ignored all the warning signs that other major things were missing or wrong and went for the one thing I thought they could give me that I so desperately wanted. With Gary, I wanted companionship, mutual love, and respect.

We had only been dating a few months when one of the folk dancers tried to convince me that because Gary was in his forties and still single, and had never been serious with anyone, that he was one of those guys who just didn't want to be in a committed relationship. This fed into my own self-doubt, and my history of making poor relationship choices. But soon I understood that it wasn't fair to judge this relationship by my past. I certainly wasn't the same person who had made those earlier choices, and I needed to discover who Gary really was and not base my opinions on what anyone else thought. Thank God, when I had doubts about whether to keep seeing him or not, Spirit kept whispering to me, and once again, I listened. I was simply afraid to allow myself to feel love again because I had been wrong so many times before. When doubts had arisen in the past, the negative messages inside me were what I listened to rather than the voice of wisdom because I didn't know how to distinguish them. This time I could sort through the muddle.

Gary seemed to really enjoy my company; he missed me when we weren't together; we laughed; we talked about important issues (like children and money). He didn't tell me he loved me right away and at first that bothered me. But with my newfound peace, I could get quiet and wait, knowing deep in my soul, that when and if Gary ever said those words to me, he would mean them forever. A deep sense of security and solidity pervaded my relationship with Gary. I felt safe and could sense the difference this time. It's the feeling all children should have about their parents and their home—that no matter what happens in the outside world, when you come home to mom and dad, everything will be all right—you're safe and you'll be taken care of. I'm not saying my relationship with Gary is adult to child—it's just that as a child I never felt safe, so for me, it was really the first time I ever had that feeling and it was and is quite delicious. With Larry, Mark, and Eddie, I'd had a false sense of security.

About seven months into the relationship, Gary invited me for a weekend at his cabin in the Pecos Wilderness in northern New Mexico. We drove there Friday night and woke up Saturday morning to an overcast sky. The wind rustled the tall pines and aspens behind the cabin while the ravens crowed their complaints from a high perch in the evergreens across the road. The plan was to hike to Hamilton Mesa and have lunch at the top, where the vistas sprawled in 360° splendor.

"I don't think it's such a good idea to hike up there today," I said. This would be the third or fourth hike for this New Yorker turned New Mexican. Hiking on a sunny day was one thing, hiking in the rain something else entirely. And in the Pecos Wilderness, in early June, one could never be sure about the weather.

"It will be fine," said Gary. The shy computer programmer from Plainview, Texas had spent his boyhood summers in this very cabin. He was quite sure of himself in the woods, not so sure of himself with people. Gary had never been in a serious relationship before.

I came out of the log cabin's only bedroom, dominated by a king-size bed. A small night stand and dead flies lining the windowsill were the only other occupants. Gary was at the kitchen table assembling the things we would need for the hike: sandwiches, water bottles, toilet paper, and rain gear—just in case.

"What's wrong with you?" I asked, noticing Gary's normally competent fingers fumbling. He couldn't seem to get the sandwiches into the opening of the bags without spilling half the contents onto the table.

"Nothing," he said, not looking at me.

That morning Gary was even quieter than usual.

"I know something's bothering you. You're acting funny," I said.

"No, Karen," he said quietly. "Everything's fine."

I walked through the kitchen into the cabin's main living area. The remnants from last night's fire were gone. Sinking into the futon, I stared at my hiking boots sitting neatly on the floor where Gary had left them for me. The breakfast dishes were done, lunch was made and packed, and Gary seemed anxious to get going. I watched out of the corner of my eye as he walked from the kitchen to the Ford Explorer outside, where he loaded the backpacks and Wolfie into what we affectionately referred to as "the Big Blue Thing."

"Come on. Let's go," Gary said, walking back into the living room.

"It's going to take several hours before we reach the top and I know you'll get hungry," he said, gently pushing the hair that had fallen into my eyes off to the side.

He tugged on my hand and I rose slowly, melting into his hug, loving the shelter of his arms. Together, we turned and walked to the car, where Wolfie panted expectantly in the back seat. During the twenty-minute drive to the trailhead at Iron Gate, we didn't speak. By the time we parked the car and strapped on our gear, the sky had darkened considerably. I looked up at the threatening clouds, about to say something, when Gary turned to me, his eyes glittering. I decided to keep my fear of the outdoors to myself.

We started up the trail, which winds around Grass Mountain and gradually gets steeper. The soft, dirt floor of the woods made the hiking easier than a concrete or gravel path, and the covering from the tall trees blanketed us from the cool breeze. Here and there, squirrels scampered up and down thick tree trunks, and we waited patiently for Wolfie to realize he couldn't catch them once they went up the tree. Every so often, we stopped to look at a vista peeking through a clump of trees or to listen to the aspen leaves whispering in the distance. About an hour into the hike, we heard the first clap of thunder.

"What's that?" I asked, knowing.

"Don't worry," Gary said. "It sounded pretty far off."

"I want to turn back," I said.

"Karen, I really want to show you the top of the mesa. Please, come with me."

The trees began to rustle more, the sky darkened even further; the path through the forest became steeper as we climbed closer to the top. It started to sprinkle.

"I want to go back," I whined, stopping yet again to look back down the trail.

Gary, who was more comfortable in the woods than anywhere else (except perhaps behind a computer screen), looked forlorn.

"We'll be okay. I promise," he said, dropping the backpack and putting his arms around me. "You'll see," he said, as he patted my back.

Another forty-five minutes and we arrived at Hamilton Mesa. Gary had hoped the sky would clear up several thousand feet higher, but when we reached the meadow, the views were blocked by dense clouds. The air was thick and moist. Blue and purple flowers were scattered around the meadow and I could smell the rain in the distance. Thunder sounded closer and closer with each clap. Even Wolfie stopped chasing squirrels and stayed by our side.

Pulling the sandwiches and drinks from the backpack, Gary placed them on the boulders we'd found for our picnic. Just as we settled down to eat, thunder roared, lightning quickly followed, and the heavens opened up, drenching the turkey sandwiches, the dog, and the two humans wanting a romantic lunch in the forest. Gary quickly gathered our things while I dashed for cover in the woods. I found a circle of trees with several fallen trunks and sat on one of the logs, shivering.

Gary came to sit beside me. "I'm sorry. I thought the rain would wait."

"Get away from me. Just leave me alone."

I didn't want to look at him; I was too angry. Huddled deep inside myself, I watched the downpour from the quasi-shelter of the woods. Suddenly a bolt of lightning hit a tree stump a few hundred yards away and I screamed. My heart was beating fast and I didn't trust myself to speak, convinced we were going to die. I didn't know much about lightning, but I knew enough to know the woods were not the best place to be.

We sat, me on one log, Gary on another, and Wolfie lying somewhere in between. Forcing myself to eat the soaked sandwich Gary placed in front of me, I wished we'd brought a thermos of hot chocolate instead of jugs filled with ice water.

"I'm sorry I shouted at you," I said.

Enough time had passed for me to calm down and let my blood sugar level even out. The rain slowed and the lightning moved off in another direction; thunder now sounded far off in the distance. We were left with the damp log, a dirt path that was now mud, and one water-logged collie with that awful wet dog smell.

"It's my fault, "Gary replied. "I shouldn't have insisted on hiking today."

Something in his voice made me look up. He was crying.

"What is it? I knew something was wrong. I felt it all morning. You're leaving me, right?" I asked.

Wiping his eyes with the corner of his sweatshirt, Gary looked at me while Wolfie watched the two of us, his large head resting on his two front paws.

"What makes you think that?" he asked.

"I wouldn't blame you if you did. I'm hateful," I said.

Gary stood up and walked to where I sat hunched over, my arms hugging my knees. He got down on one knee, reached over and lifted my chin so we were eye to eye.

"I'm not leaving you, Karen. Let's head back down the mountain," he said.

Later that night, after a quiet dinner and an evening curled up in front of the fire reading, we cuddled in bed. Gary drew me close, spooning.

"Karen, the reason I insisted we go up the mountain today is because I wanted to tell you something," he whispered. "I wanted to say "I love you," and I wanted to say it for the first time someplace special to me. I'm so sorry."

In that tender moment I knew this was how I wanted to be loved. Though I had no way of knowing whether our relationship would last, I knew that Gary was worth the risk of trying.

* * *

Summer 1995

Shortly after our weekend in Pecos, I went to see my folks in Florida, a trip I made once a year. With the intense heat and high humidity, breathing outdoors was difficult. The three of us sat in my parent's air-conditioned living room watching TV, just as we had when I was growing up. That night, the phone rang and my mother answered it. A few minutes later I heard her say, "David, your mother is here. Do you want to talk to her?" The next thing I knew, she handed me the receiver.

My heart felt as if it had stopped, but I managed to register that David seemed glad we were talking. A lump grew in my throat when he told me he had recently graduated from college and wanted to come see me; he needed answers to questions about my divorce from his father. I said he could come any time he wanted.

When I returned home from Florida, I shared with Gary my concern about David's pending visit.

"It will be so awkward staying in the same house after so many years," I said.

Gary and I had been talking about moving in together, so he suggested David stay in my apartment for the last few weeks of my lease and that I move into Gary's house. It was an elegant solution.

Late one night, David arrived at my apartment where I waited, alone. When I opened the door, I could not believe my eyes. David had grown to over six feet tall and was rail thin with long dark hair and a beard. Pain filled his brown eyes as he bent to put his arms around me. I'd last hugged a seventeen-year-old boy. Now my arms were wrapped around a twenty-two-year-old man.

After driving across the country David was exhausted, but wanted to talk anyway. Sitting across from one another at my kitchen table, David leaned forward, his long legs sprawled to the side. I sat hunched over the table, my fingers clutched tightly around my teacup.

He shared intimately with me that night, exposing truths I had never known. He said that as a child he had "absorbed" his father and Carol's feelings towards me and that is what caused him to keep emotionally distant. David said it didn't have anything to do with not loving me, but he understood how it appeared. Our talk went till the wee hours of the morning that first night, with David asking tough questions. It was the first time he heard my perspective on the divorce and subsequent custody battle, and he appeared shell-shocked.

Words and time spans jumped all over the map as he attempted to fill me in on his life, his voice raised at times, and a whisper at others. Listening and answering as best as I could, I tried not to paint a false picture. I could feel the emotional pain David carried in every cell in my body. All I wanted to do was grab him and rock the pain away. But I'd lost that opportunity years ago, and now all I could do was be fully present for my grown-up child.

"Why did you leave me when I was four-years-old?" he asked.

Holding nothing back, I told him the story. For the first time, David heard that I didn't leave; he had been taken from me. I was surprised to learn that this earlier experience plagued him more than my moving away from New York when he was eleven. That night we started the process of healing and re-connecting. When I got home to Gary, I told him it would take time to get to know and understand my son. I was so afraid he would pick up and run again before we could permanently bond.

I waited a few days before introducing David to Gary, but they had an ease with one another right from the start. David especially got a kick out of the fact that he grew up in Plainview, Long Island and Gary grew up in Plainview, Texas.

One day, friends of ours called inviting us to participate in a sweat lodge ceremony. I had attended sweat lodges while living in Oregon, but neither Gary nor David had. Eager to try something so out of the ordinary, David agreed immediately. Gary was a bit nervous, however, but willing to come anyway. During the ceremony, each participant has an opportunity to offer up prayers to the Great Spirit. As the people shared around the circle, I was moved to ask for healing for my son and me. I truly don't remember what else I said, but months later, Gary told me it was in that sweat lodge that he realized he wanted to spend the rest of his life with me.

Three weeks into David's stay, he came over to our house for dinner. That evening, David excused himself after the meal and went to make a phone call. Gary and I took Wolfie for a walk and when we returned, David said, "Mom, my Dad wants to talk to you."

Larry and I hadn't spoken in more than a decade. Ellen was on the extension line and the three of us talked for quite a while. They told me David was a troubled young man who had been difficult all his life. He was sullen with them, and arrogant, saying and doing what he wanted, disregarding others' feelings. That is how he seemed to me as well, yet at times during this particular visit, he was also sensitive and perceptive. I listened to what they had to say, but decided to make up my own mind about who David had been and who he had become.

When David left for New York, he promised that the past few weeks together had just been the beginning of our reunion. The process of communicating with David, as well as with Larry and Ellen, helped me begin to believe there wasn't anything wrong with me, and nothing I should or shouldn't have done to make things right. Slowly, the guilt and negative self-talk which had previously convinced me I was an irresponsible monster who had abandoned my child began to lift.

* * *

One Saturday morning two weeks after David left, I woke up to find Gary in the kitchen making breakfast.

"Good morning," I said, walking over to hug him.

"Hey," he said, but his usual warm smile was missing.

"Anything the matter?" I asked.

"No."

"You sure?"

"Yes."

"Okay," I said, deciding to drop it. After showering and getting dressed, I sank onto the couch in the living room to read. Gary was out walking Wolfie. I couldn't shake the feeling something was wrong. *He can't handle my moods. The insanity of my former life is too much for him. He's had it; he's going to break up with me.*

"How was your walk?" I asked.

"Fine."

"Look, something is the matter, I just know it," I said.

Gary glanced over and shook his head no.

I rested my head on my knees. A few minutes later I felt Gary's hand on my hair. As I looked up, I saw Gary's face in front of mine, tears streaming down it. He was on one knee.

"Karen," he whispered. "Will you marry me?"

I began to cry, not answering right away. *I guess my intuition was right—something was going on—I just assumed it was something bad.*

He asked me again.

"Yes," I whispered, wrapping my arms around him. Both of us were crying as Gary explained that the ring he had chosen was at the jeweler being sized and that was why he had been acting weird. He was trying to decide when and how to ask me once he picked up the ring.

"I hope some day you'll trust my love," Gary said, when we had both settled down. I couldn't believe he wasn't angry at me for spoiling his proposal. Instead, he was concerned for me. My spirit inched one step closer towards wholeness. Later that day, we phoned family and friends with our good news.

* * *

125

Two months after David's New Mexico visit, he phoned asking me to come to New York. He wanted to bring his entire family together for a meeting. My intestines danced a jig as I thought about facing Larry, Ellen, and Carol after all these years. But at the same time, I wanted to do whatever I could to help David heal.

On a blistering cold day in early December, Gary stayed in our motel room while I drove the snow-lined streets of Plainview to Larry and Ellen's house. Gary had convinced me not to make this trip alone, but we both agreed it wasn't appropriate for him to participate in this meeting.

It was late afternoon when we gathered in their den, and I found myself sitting on my old furniture—the same brown and white striped sofa bed, the same brown recliner, the same stereo cabinet I'd left eighteen years before.

Larry had gained a considerable amount of weight, as had Ellen. With his black hair mostly gray, he no longer looked like John Lennon.

David sat between Larry and me on the sofa, Ellen in the recliner, and Carol and her husband in chairs across the room. I barely glanced at Carol, but noticed she still had long hair, now streaked with gray. She was dressed much like her mother had dressed, in a tailored suit and heavy make-up. David turned to me.

"I don't remember a time when I sat between my parents."

Reaching over, I put my arm around him, thinking how David's childhood had been damaged much like mine had been—different scenarios, but similar results. Fortunately, he exhibited more self-confidence and wisdom than I had at his age. Still, my heart ached for all this now grown man had lost because of his parents' behavior. Tears threatened to spill out, but I held them back. Sitting on the couch next to the ex-husband who had hurt me so deeply, I felt vulnerable and wanted to protect myself. I tried to stay present as David released his pent-up feelings, expressing his anger for being placed in the position of having to choose between his parents. He also talked about how painful choosing had been. Then he put his arm around me.

"This is my Mom and I am not willing to tolerate your hatred of her any longer," he said to his father, but his words were meant for everyone in the room. "I want her in my life."

126

He went on to say he wanted everyone he loved to be in his life without anger and hostility and that's what he expected from then on. By this time I couldn't hold the tears back any longer. David asked if I had anything to say and I mumbled something about how hard it had been to lose all of them and David at the same time. Then it was over.

Sobbing, I drove back to the motel, remembering another drive oh so long ago after I'd been served the restraining order. This time, however, Gary waited for me with open arms and a loving heart. Gently, he wiped my tears and stroked my back as I shared what happened.

"It's all right, Karen. Shh. Everything will be okay now," he whispered. The next morning we flew home to New Mexico.

Though Carol had had little to say to me, and Ellen nothing at all, that afternoon gathering began a partial healing between Larry and me. We started to periodically call each other, and during one of those conversations Larry said, "There was nothing you could have done to make our marriage work, Karen. It wasn't your fault; no one could have made me happy back then."

* * *

February 1996

Two months later, David flew in for our wedding. Despite the blustery wind that frequently blows in Albuquerque in February, more than one hundred guests arrived, including forty folk dancers. Since Gary had never been married, he'd wanted a real wedding with a church ceremony as well as a reception with dinner and dancing. Gary had grown up Episcopalian and even though it had been years since I'd attended a service, I was comfortable with Gary's minister. He agreed to remove the name "Jesus" from the service and replace it with "God." He even incorporated my Jewish background into our ceremony.

One friend played the organ while another sang as the wedding party walked down the aisle. I waited at the back of the church for Mary Alice, my Matron of Honor, to reach the front. Then, with my dad holding one arm and David the other, I walked towards Gary, waiting at the altar. Neither Gary nor I could stop smiling as the minister pronounced us husband and wife. And when we proceeded down the aisle and Gary's

127

mom said, "Welcome to the family, Mrs. Walker," the entire congregation heard me shriek with joy.

People still talk about our reception. Aside from scrumptious food and ever-flowing champagne, we surprised my parents with a 50th anniversary wedding cake and had the DJ play "Oh, How We Danced on the Night We Were Wed" for them. At one point in the evening, the DJ called for quiet. He said, "At this time, David, the bride's son, has a special gift for his mother and Gary."

David smiled at me as he walked to the front of the head table, sat down on a chair the DJ had provided, and picked up his guitar.

"I want you to know how happy I am to be here," he said to the crowd. "It's so great, meeting Gary's family for the first time."

Laughing, he described how overwhelming it was—the same reaction I'd had—Gary's family is huge. Then he spoke about the Plainview connection he and Gary had while he softly strummed his guitar. He sang a U-2 hit called "*The First Time.*" As I listened to David sing and looked out at the circle of friends and family, many of whom knew our history, there wasn't a dry eye to be seen. When David finished, he stood up, walked over to where Gary and I were hanging on to each other, both crying hard, and put his arms around us both. Later that evening, Gary and I smiled as we watched David attempt some folk dances. Although awkward and unsure of himself, he was giggling, not afraid to fully enjoy the celebration. At 2:00 am we were all still dancing.

* * *

February 1997

One year after our wedding, Carol died.

"Mom, I want you to come but I'm conflicted," David said when he called to tell me. "I'm concerned others will be uncomfortable, but I need you here. I'm pissed that this is still an issue."

"So am I," I said.

Larry's family had been uncomfortable with me ever since the divorce. My hunch was it was too awkward to explain to others who I was. If I wasn't around, they could pretend they were a normal family. In the end, though, David's desire to have me there for comfort won out and I went back to New York. David made arrangements for me to ride with one of his closest friends. It was odd spending time with someone David had grown up with. I wondered what he thought of a woman who was David's mom but hadn't been involved in his life.

After the funeral, we all went back to Carol's house. It was strange being in a place I had not been invited to when she was alive. Standing in the central hallway, I stared at pictures of the girl I had once loved so much. Wedding pictures were displayed as well, but none with me in them, although I'd been there. Photographs of her now teen-aged sons as babies dominated the wall. I was glad she had been able to conceive and carry a child to term. During her Hodgkin's treatments, she'd been told she might never have children.

In that moment I began to grieve the loss of the childhood best friend who had abandoned me. Later, David told me he could see in my face what the loss of those I had loved so deeply had done to me. By the time Carol died, Margaret, Grammy and Poppy were gone as well. At Carol's gravesite earlier that day, I'd said the goodbyes I'd not had the opportunity to say before.

Just before leaving Carol's house, I sat at the kitchen table with Carol's husband, Larry and Ellen, and David. Listening to Ellen refer to Carol's boys as "my nephews" I watched the dynamics of the family members I'd lost. Pieces of my broken heart mended that day, but I was unable to ask the question that still haunted me—how Larry went for custody the way he did without ever attempting to speak to me about it and why he had lied to a judge. I did not have the courage to bring up the custody issue, nor was I sure I should, either that day or any other day. As of this writing, I still haven't done so. I don't want to jeopardize the cordiality that now exists. David had asked for peace so that when events occur in which all of David's family attends, it wouldn't be uncomfortable. I wanted that for him then and still do.

* * *

1998

"Hi Mom," said David, speaking my two favorite words in the English language. It was about nine o'clock Sunday morning and for the past few months David had called around this time almost every week.

"What are you doing today?" I asked.

"Playing street hockey," he said. My stomach clutched in a familiar way.

"I wish I was there to watch."

My guilt had been gradually lessening as David and I built a relationship, the protective coating around my heart slowly wearing off. But as it did, the pain of the loss felt like being flattened by a steam roller. I'd missed his school years, meetings with teachers, having his friends over, his first girlfriend, his high school graduation, and college years. Emotions surrounding those losses had been buried, but were suddenly bubbling up. Yet I now understood that David had lost out as well. Even though Ellen was a good stepmother to him, she could not take the place of his mom.

Towards the end of 1998, David came for a visit. He had something he wanted to talk about. The day after he arrived, he and I went to the Bosque—a green oasis of land overgrown with old Cottonwood trees and dense foliage that stretches for miles along the Rio Grande river. It had been about two years since David had walked back into my life.

Hiking a ways, we found a lovely spot by the river where the water whooshed past us as we sat on a fallen cottonwood log. David munched an apple while I guzzled water, both content to soak in the beauty of the Bosque. I was anxious to know what David wanted to talk about, but knew enough to let him do it in his own time and in his own way. He said he was going for a short walk and I nodded, pulling out my journal. As always, writing down my feelings soothed my turbulent emotions.

When David returned about a half hour later, he sat opposite me on the log, leaned forward, and took my hands in his.

"I'm so glad you're in my life, Mom," David said. "You don't need to do anything to win my approval or my love. You have it. I know you did things that hurt me, but I know now it wasn't intentional. I forgive you. Let it go. Let's just move forward from now on."

Until then, Mother's Day had been the saddest day of the year for me. But now, the boy who had been ripped out of my arms was back where he belonged. It had been twenty-two years since the day I was served the restraining order. Yet, even though my son had spoken magical words which helped release some of my guilt, it still would be years before I could completely forgive myself.

One additional barrier, though, remained between my son and me. During one of our weekly phone conversations a few months after the forgiveness visit, David confessed that he was worried about his school loans. That first night in New Mexico, he'd told me he resented the fact that I didn't participate in his growing up, particularly financially, so I knew this was an issue for him. Logically, he understood that I didn't contribute because of what happened and because he stopped speaking to me, but emotionally, he was never satisfied.

"How much are they?" I asked.

"Ten thousand dollars."

Gary and I had talked about this right after David came back into my life, and he told me he'd support whatever decision I made to help my son. Part of my guilt came from feeling irresponsible as a parent for not helping to pay for David's college tuition. I'd told Gary that regardless of the reasons, parents have a responsibility to educate their children and I hadn't done that.

"David, I'm going to put a check in the mail today to pay off your loan," I said.

He was speechless.

"This is not a loan. It is not a gift. It is simply my way to atone for my lack of responsibility."

I believe somehow, that gesture sutured the rift remaining between us. It didn't mean we wouldn't have difficult times ahead or that our relationship would be idyllic. I knew better. But we knew we loved one another and that he had a mom and step dad in Gary who would be there for him no matter what.

* * *

Some time after I drafted this section of the memoir, I turned on *The Oprah Winfrey* show. The topic that day was women and how they felt about motherhood. Women talked about not feeling fulfilled; women felt overwhelmed; they were depressed; women couldn't emotionally handle staying home with children. Listening to them was a balm on my soul—there were millions more out there who felt the same way I had. Gratitude filled my heart—women were now free to tell the truth.

131

As I heard women share feelings no one had dared utter when I was a new mom, my inner healing spread even further. *Perhaps I wasn't a freak of nature after all.*

With the wisdom that comes with age and a great deal of therapy, I could put in perspective the events which had converged after giving birth. David and I had not been together for three days after his birth. And because of my gall bladder surgery several weeks after the caesarian, we missed other opportunities for the mother/child bonding to occur. My depression after his birth further distanced us. Losing custody ensured that distance would only increase.

I used to regret having a child because I felt I had failed so miserably at motherhood. But today I am grateful for my son. Despite the rough time he had growing up, he's turned out to be a wonderful person—one whom I love, respect and admire. I recently told him that even if we weren't related, he is someone I would want to know. He's looked at his own childhood, examined his relationships with me and other family members, in therapy and on his own. And I know that because of the issues he's resolved, if and when he has children, he will hand down a much stronger, more loving legacy than the one he received.

* * *

Chapter 11

My Father's Keeper

<u>July 2001</u>

"Oh my God," I said to my mother when I walked into their Century Village condo, located in Deerfield Beach, Florida.

"I can't take it anymore. I'm ready to go to the other side," Mom said.

Nothing new here; Mom had always been dramatic. But this time, I understood. My eighty-six-year-old father was covered with red, puss-filled sores over most of his body. Sitting on the same old couch in the dark living room with the faded yellow shag carpeting with his chin pressed far into his chest, he looked so shrunken he could disappear into the mint green fabric with the yellow daisies. He seemed withered inside himself, his hideous rash screaming for attention.

"Dad," I said, "you poor thing."

He raised his chin slightly. Those mischievous brown eyes of his were tiny slits, covered with scabs.

"Hi, baby," he said, looking up, then quickly putting his head back down.

It was hard to see this once vibrant man so shriveled and old. His once thick, black hair was now thin and white. Nothing had prepared me for this, as I'd physically and emotionally distanced myself from my parents since I'd married Larry at nineteen. When they moved to Florida

133

in 1975, I limited my visits to once or twice a year, and each time, I witnessed them a bit frailer, a little slower, and less alert. But this kind of deterioration was unexpected. My cousin Richard, who lives in Florida, had called suggesting I make this trip. He'd said the skin condition my Dad had been suffering from for the past six months had gotten worse and he didn't think my mother knew what to do about it.

"Madeline, it hurts. You're not doing it right. Goddamn it, you're hurting me," Dad screamed, as Mom applied prescription medications to his skin.

"I'm trying, Bill," she said.

"I'm sorry. I just can't stand it."

That night, I lay awake on the pull-out bed in the den next to their bedroom listening as I had as a child, alternating between thinking their yelling was staged for my benefit and believing it was my fault. I wanted to help them but was unable to intrude on their nightly dance of misery.

What I could do was take Dad from physician to physician, trying to determine what was wrong. At the same time, I'd begun to notice my mother squinting, barely missing curbs, and unable to read street signs while driving. After a bit of coaxing, she agreed to have the cataract surgery her eye doctor had recently recommended.

On August 9th, three weeks after I'd arrived in Florida, Mom and I woke up at 5:00 am. Her surgery was scheduled for 6:30 that morning. It went smoothly and we got home just in time for me to take Dad to a highly recommended dermatologist. For some reason, Dad kissed Mom goodbye when we left, an odd sight.

"Your dad has an auto-immune disease," the young doctor explained. "His body thinks his skin is 'foreign,' and is attacking it. Plus, he has a serious staph infection. We need to hospitalize him immediately."

Thank God. Finally, a physician who knows how to treat Dad. I phoned Mom to fill her in and make sure she was okay, even though I had asked a neighbor to look in on her. I wasn't particularly worried. After all, cataract surgery is a straightforward procedure.

It took seven hours to get Dad admitted to the hospital. At 9:00 pm that night, I left Dad asleep in his hospital room. My body ached and I felt as if I were dragging an elephant behind me. Now that we finally had a diagnosis and treatment plan, I could let go a little. When I walked in

134

the door, Mom was sitting on the couch, surprisingly calm and smiling. Leaning down, I gave her a hug.

"Would you like to sleep with me tonight?" she asked. I'd been complaining that the sofa bed in the den was uncomfortable.

"No thanks, Mom," I said, bending to kiss her goodnight. "I'm whipped and I'm sure I'll sleep better by myself. I'm going to bed." I walked down the hall and into my room, where I promptly fell into an exhausted sleep.

The next morning I woke up early, not bothering to check on Mom; she often slept late. I phoned David to let him know about Grandpa's status and asked if he wanted to come for a visit. He said he'd think about it. Then I walked down the hall to the kitchen to grab a glass of orange juice.

As I walked back to my room, I could see Mom lying on her back, her right arm hanging down the side of the bed. *What an odd position.* I walked in and stood over the bed. Her un-patched eye stared up at the ceiling.

"Mom," I said, gently rubbing her shoulder, but there was no response.

I placed my hand on her chest. She wasn't breathing

"This can't be happening!" I screamed as I ran out the door to get Mom's neighbor. Barbara came back with me, took one look at Mom and said, "You better call 911."

My ability to compartmentalize my emotions came in handy. While Barbara and I waited for the paramedics, I made phone calls, phoning David first because, after our conversation earlier that morning, he needed to know Grandma had died, not Grandpa. I needed Gary next, but he was at folk dance camp and unreachable by phone. I knew my friend Grace was leaving for camp that day, so despite the fact that it was only 6:00 am in Albuquerque, I phoned her with the news and asked her to please have Gary call me.

About an hour later, the paramedics arrived. After a brief examination, they came out to the living room and said, "She died sometime during the night. It appears to be natural causes."

They told me the Medical Examiner's office would be by later that morning to retrieve the body. I closed the door to Mom's room, and told Barbara I was okay for now; she could go home. Then I spent the next few hours phoning Social Security, Medicare, Dad's postal employee insurance company, as well as relatives and Mom's friends. It was early afternoon when I sat on the couch in my parents' living room and watched as the stretcher carrying my mother was wheeled out the door.

No time to grieve. Dad waited at the hospital. How was I going to tell him? He'd had several small strokes over the last few years. The skin disease and infection had further weakened him. I was afraid he'd have a heart attack or a more serious stroke.

"Where's Madeline?" Dad asked as I walked in.

"She's resting, Dad," I explained. *Not a total lie.* Several minutes later after the sedative the doctor had agreed to administer had taken effect, I was able to tell him about Mom.

For a moment, the jarring news didn't seem to register with Dad. Then his eyes went moist and closed. "Oh no, it should have been me," he said.

"Mom was really happy last night. She knew you were finally going to be okay."

He didn't cry. I wasn't sure if the sedative prevented emotional responses, but I was grateful he stayed calm.

"How long will I have to be here?" Dad asked.

"We don't know yet," I said, as I explained his diagnosis and treatment plan.

"I had a really good breakfast this morning. Orange juice, scrambled eggs, potatoes, a bagel and coffee," he said.

"That's great," I responded. "Is there a game on today?"

"Yeah, the Yankees are playing the Cubs."

"Well, Dad, I've got to go. Lots to take care of. Enjoy the game, okay?"

"Okay," he said, already flipping the channels on the remote control.

I left the hospital and took care of more details relating to Mom's death. That night I sat down in their living room to think. After relegating my parents to once-a-year visits and weekly phone calls, I suddenly faced full-time responsibility for my elderly, ill, now widowed father.

It no longer mattered that I had grown up hating myself as a result of this man's verbal abuse. He was my father; I was his only child. I phoned my husband, who had come home from camp as soon as he heard my news, and told him I couldn't leave our life in New Mexico to stay in Florida to care for my father. I explained that Dad could no longer negotiate the stairs, drive a car, or care for himself.

"It's possible to hire someone to stay with him, but I have visions of too many flights back and forth. I just don't think that's a viable solution. The best thing is to bring him back to New Mexico," I said.

"We can clean out the pool table room for Dad," Gary said. "It's downstairs and near a bathroom we don't use ourselves, so he could have his own wing."

After talking it through a bit more, we agreed that Gary would get the room ready and then come out to help drive us all back to New Mexico. David also volunteered to help as well. There was to be no funeral or memorial service for my mother; she had not wanted one.

Dad remained in the hospital for nine more days at which point I was able to bring him home to his condo. The next morning, we went to the bank. After that, we were going to scatter Mom's ashes somewhere on the grounds of their retirement community. I had picked them up the day before; they were in a cardboard container in a shopping bag in the trunk of Dad's car. But Dad behaved strangely at the bank. He kept nodding off as we sat at the bank officer's desk and barely managed to scrawl his name on the necessary papers. In no shape to deal with Mom's ashes, I helped him up the stairs and settled him in a chair in the living room. A few minutes later, I walked over and asked if he was feeling better.

He slurred a response.

Dad's eyes looked vacant, so I ran to the kitchen and phoned 911. Twenty minutes later, paramedics were wheeling my father out the door on a stretcher. They told me I could follow them to the hospital.

In Dad's car, I trailed the ambulance for a few blocks. *Oh my God, Mom's ashes are in the trunk of the car.* Unable to stand the thought of her remains in the trunk while Dad was being whisked to the hospital, I swerved the car into a U-turn and drove to the funeral parlor a few blocks away. Grabbing the shopping bag out of the trunk, I walked into the office and slammed the bag on the desk saying, "You deal with this. I can't. Whatever she said to do with her, just do it," and walked back out to the car.

At that moment I was a volcano ready to erupt, furious with my mother for leaving me to deal with Dad and terrified he was going to die on me, just like she did. I'd not had a second to process anything that had happened since I'd arrived in Florida. I was desperate to write in my journal, but had no time.

At the emergency room, I was told my Dad had had what is called a TIA, a mild stroke, and needed to remain in the hospital for a few days for observation. That made it easier for me to prepare for Dad's move to New Mexico. I put their condominium on the market and began sorting through my parents' belongings. As I packed my mother's pewter hair brush and the plastic hand which sat on her dresser wearing her various rings, I cried silent tears for the woman who'd gotten her wish—she was now "on the other side."

By the time Dad came home from the hospital, all the boxes which would go to New Mexico were labeled, and the rest of the furniture and belongings had been given to various charitable organizations.

The morning before David and Gary were to arrive, I left Dad watching TV in the den, got in the car and drove to Deerfield Beach. The heat of the day had not yet reached its peak and the beach was fairly deserted. Waves gently lapped the shore, and the sand felt cool on my bare feet. My mother had not wanted a funeral, but I needed to honor her passing. I sat cross-legged on the sand, facing the ocean, my hands resting palms up on my knees. With eyes closed, I asked Spirit to guide my mother's soul to a place where she might finally have peace. It was only then my tears flowed. She'd gotten what she'd said she wanted. Maybe now my mother would finally be happy.

* * *

September 2001

Two months had passed since I'd arrived in Florida to assist Mom with Dad's illness. David and Gary helped with the final moving arrangements. We rented a U-haul and attached it to Dad's Toyota Camry. It took hours to pack the truck and in the end, we had to leave a dresser behind. On September 1, we left Florida to begin the four-day journey that would bring Dad home to New Mexico. My life would now revolve around caring for my father. David stayed for a few days to help get his Grandpa settled, but he had to get back to work.

138

With Mom gone and Dad so ill, I was forced to spend time with him I had never imagined necessary. At first, I was hyper-vigilant, watching him every second. When I couldn't fall asleep, I'd get up and walk into his room to see if he was still breathing, unable to rid myself of the image of my mother lying in bed, her blank stare focused up, not breathing. The little girl inside me, the one who had sometimes wished her parents dead or that she'd been born into another family, was going to make sure she didn't find her father the same way. This was countered by the adult who resented having to care for the man who had made her childhood so miserable.

I was also grieving for my mom, wishing I'd been able to spend that last day with her, wishing I'd had the energy to talk with her more that night. The medical examiner said there was no cause of death—her heart, lungs, kidneys and liver were fine. It wasn't the cataract surgery. There'd been no adverse reaction to the anesthesia. It just happened. She had gone to sleep and hadn't awakened. I didn't get to say goodbye and neither did she. But my grief was mostly about how unhappy she'd been for as long as I'd known her. And for the mother I'd needed as a child but didn't have. I had to come to terms with the fact that it was her life; she'd made her choices and experienced her destiny. The challenge for me was with my still living father. To not allow the way he speaks and the way he behaves to undermine all the growth I'd achieved.

An occupational therapist came three times a week to teach Dad how to get out of bed, put his socks on with the aid of a device, sit up from a reclining position, and stand from a seated position. Twice a week a nurse arrived to check Dad's skin, blood pressure and oxygen levels. As the skin condition healed, the scabs scattered in Dad's wake, driving me nuts. Luckily for me, his limited mobility kept him confined to a small space consisting of his room, the bathroom, and the dining room.

We slipped into a daily routine.

"Good morning, Dad," I said as I helped him make his way to the dining room table.

"Damn it. I still can't get used to this walker," he said.

"It'll take time," I replied.

He'd slowly sip his juice, eat his cereal and toast, then drink his coffee. "Gary's waiting to help you shower and dress," I said, when he finished. I drew the line at seeing Dad naked. Next, I'd rub the creams and ointments on him and dress his wounds in gauze.

"I'm such a burden," he moaned, staring down at his feet.

"No, you're not, Dad," I'd lie. My heart sagged inside my chest, weighed down with guilt for not feeling loving towards him, as "a good daughter" should.

After Gary left for work, I headed upstairs to our home office to do my school work. A few years after Gary and I had married, a long-buried dream had surfaced—a dream which had started when I was a little girl and wanted to be a writer, just like Jo in *Little Women*. But I had scarcely admitted that dream to myself, let alone anyone else. In the first few months of our marriage, I whispered this dream to my new husband Gary in the quiet times of our getting to know each other. Three years later, he provided me with financial support so I could write full time.

From 1999, when I quit working, to 2001, I poured through the journals I'd been keeping since 1978 and drafted what turned out to be a self-help book. When I hired an editor, however, she said that I had a book in me, but it wasn't on those pages. She told me that I just needed to "tell my story." But I didn't know how to do that.

At the same time, I realized I still had some shame around never completing my college education. For thirty-two years I had vacillated between wanting to finish college and thinking it wasn't worth it. Education had not been a priority in my family and there was always some reason not to go after I'd left home. Finally, after all those years of ignoring the niggling voices inside my head that made me feel bad about not having the degree, I decided to do something about it.

The steps leading to admission at the University of New Mexico (UNM) were challenging. My ancient transcripts were on microfiche somewhere in the bowels of Queensborough Community College in New York. After weeks of letters and phone conversations, one angel of a clerk sent them to UNM. *Great. I'm admitted.* Then more hoops to jump through before my credits from the 1960's could be counted towards my degree. Finally, with fifty credits to my name, I registered for fall semester in the University Studies program where I could take as many Creative Writing courses as I wanted. Completing the degree and writing were both long held dreams I hadn't even allowed myself to think about, even though writing had proven to be a profound method for me to connect with my innermost feelings and speak my truth. It was the primary tool to awaken my sleeping soul and shift from auto pilot to conscious awareness after losing custody of David.

That first day, I arrived at school, heart pounding, palms wet, hoping the agile young folks striding purposefully around school would hardly notice the dumpy, middle-aged woman with the only rolling backpack on campus. Having successfully made it from the parking lot to the shuttle to the Duck Pond, I sat discreetly on an empty bench, happy to commiserate with the honking geese and ducks. I felt like honking right along with them. But instead, I furtively glanced up, watching for anyone who might have a rolling backpack so I wouldn't feel so damned conspicuous. When it was finally time for my first class, I was convinced everyone I passed was snickering at me.

I found a seat in the corner, thinking how much worse this was than when I was nineteen. Back then, even though I felt like a misfit, no one knew because I looked the same as everyone else. Now I'm older than most of the students in class as well as the teacher. *Breathe, Karen, breathe.*

I got through that first day and the days after that, but school consumed my life. If I wasn't in classes, I was studying or writing papers. Dad's needs took second place to writing my first fiction piece ever. Making dinner took third place to learning about the consequences of fossil fuels on the environment. Yet I started to feel more assimilated and did far better in my first semester than I thought possible. When I registered for spring classes, I had a new confidence in my student persona—until I found myself in one of the core requirements classes—Astronomy.

One particular day, I felt like crying though I didn't know why. It was difficult for me to understand the math and physics theories the teacher was explaining and suddenly I was back in Mr. Plotkin's seventh grade Algebra class, convinced I was the only kid not getting it. Memories of all the times I was confused and couldn't speak up bubbled inside me. Deciding to go back to school at fifty-three had been difficult enough. I didn't expect to have to deal with unresolved issues from childhood as well.

What had I gotten myself into? My menopausal mind wasn't as sharp as it used to be. My back hurt frequently. What if my father had a crisis? Dad has health issues all the time, each one potentially serious. I never knew when I would have to drop everything and deal with something or other. I was an idiot for even thinking I could do this.

Then I remembered sitting in Mrs. Mickenberg's class in third grade. She was explaining long division. I didn't understand, couldn't concentrate, and was unable to raise my hand. It became clear to me that, growing up, I had felt shell-shocked most of the time, at home as well as at school. My parents' fights and the resulting tension pervading our household had created a need in me to block out the anger, so I'd shut down, frozen inside myself. I went through elementary, junior high, and high school in a trance, making average grades despite my emotional handicap. Now, all these years later, I finally understood why school had been so difficult. At this current time in my life, it didn't have to be that way. Instead of sitting frozen in my seat, afraid to speak, afraid to ask questions, my hand shot up frequently when I didn't understand or when I knew the answer to a question.

After making Dean's List every semester, I realized I was smarter than I've always believed myself to be. Back in school as an older adult, I could recognize destructive patterns and behavior and move past them. I felt no regrets about what could have or should have happened if things had been different. My parents did the best they could and so did I. Maybe that's why those voices had whispered for me to return to school. So I could heal some childhood wounds.

But my full life, my desire to write, and caring for my aging father competed with the need for a college degree. By the time I finished, I would be almost sixty. My time for family, writing, and friends would be shortened by required school work. When the war in Iraq started and two friends were diagnosed with life-threatening illnesses, I seriously questioned how to best spend my remaining time on Earth. Life is fragile. None of us know how long we have to live. As I struggled with balancing the key elements in my life, I wondered: If life is graded, when I get to the end, will I feel like I deserve an Incomplete? If I leave school, will I sabotage a long-held goal, or will I free myself to pursue my dream of writing? Can I do both at once? One thing was certain. It wasn't the degree that was left unfinished thirty-two years ago. It was me. I still had much to learn.

* * *

Each day, Dad settled down in his new, blue, heavily-cushioned electric recliner to watch TV, switching between ballgames, game shows and CNN. Once or twice a week I'd take him to the VA to see his internist, his eye doctor or his dermatologist. Dad loved these excursions. Always the extrovert, he'd wear his "Big Red One" hat and talk to the people around him while we waited. He sought out patients in wheelchairs or those who seemed to be alone. One time he actually offered to give someone his cane, thinking he didn't need it anymore.

"Did you hear if they caught Osama Bin Laden?" he asked a veteran one day.

"Not yet," the man said.

"Ain't that something?" said Dad.

This was mid-November 2001 and it was only now Dad understood that America had been attacked. Before this, he couldn't comprehend much of what was going on in the world or in his own life. We had only been in New Mexico about a week when the twin towers were hit. The morning of September 11th he barely registered what was occurring. He was in too much pain from his skin disease and too out of touch as a result of the strokes. He had yet to mention my mother.

I tried to maintain a semblance of the life I'd had prior to Dad's arrival. I purchased a cell phone so he could call at a moment's notice, my life squeezed between my father's needs. Gary and I folk danced Saturday nights; I went to school on Tuesdays and Thursdays with the cell phone attached to my hip. I pretended everything was okay, but secretly dreaded the sound of his walker scraping our beautiful tile floor, knowing I'd have to sweep up the scabs later. My stomach turned inside out at the sound of his voice.

"Karen. I need help," he bellowed from downstairs.

"What's the matter?" I asked, thinking he'd fallen or something.

"I dropped the remote control and can't reach it," he said.

"Goddamn it," I said, handing him the remote. "You need anything else?"

"No, thank you. I'm sorry to bother you," he mumbled.

I had few escape valves. The feelings I'd learned to manage so well during short visits to Florida now threatened to explode at any moment. Ripped apart, I wondered how love, hatred, anger and compassion could live inside me at the same time. Which would win? I tried to be patient, but didn't always succeed. Boundaries weren't just crossed, they were trampled. The past six years with Gary had been the happiest in my life.

I was in a loving relationship, with healthy give and take, and mutual respect. With my spirit at peace, I felt secure. But now my needs were being ignored as they had been as a child. I was an adult and still couldn't communicate with my father. He was too frail, too needy, too old. The child inside me who had lived in fear of this man took over. I spent my time lost in books, or shut up alone in my room, or stuffing my face, old familiar choices that once had comforted me. Again, I stopped dancing and doing other things which filled me with joy. Gary grew concerned and thought maybe I should see a therapist. I agreed.

"There are options other than having your Dad live with you," Mary said.

She was a grandmotherly type, and as she spoke, she smoothed back her shiny, gray hair and leaned forward.

"Karen," Mary said. "Although you may want to, you cannot replace everything your father lost or missed in his life."

Dad was completely isolated in our home, television his only companion while I worked upstairs or went out. Slowly, as days stretched into weeks and weeks into months, I re-evaluated the situation. In the beginning, with Mom's sudden death and with Dad still so ill, I'd felt I had no choice but to have Dad live with us. But as Dad recovered some of his strength, Mary helped me see it wasn't my responsibility to spend so much time with him if my emotional well being was threatened.

"If you make sure your Dad's basic needs are met and he isn't being abused or neglected, then that is where your responsibility ends," Mary said. "What you do above and beyond that is your choice."

Four months after bringing Dad to New Mexico, Gary and I made the decision to move him to an assisted living facility. It proved to be a good decision for Dad as well as for us. As his health improved, he made friends, joined a weekly poker game, and started playing bingo. One day, in the car on the way to the VA, he said, "I miss Madeline sometimes, but mostly, I don't. It's so peaceful now. No more fighting."

"I'm sorry you and Mom were so unhappy," I said.

"I'm just glad you found Gary and you're finally happy," he replied.

One day I was in the middle of a difficult portion of an essay, trying to wrap my mind around an idea, when the phone jingled, wrenching me out of the piece. I still couldn't bring myself to turn the ringer off, afraid I'd miss his call or miss the facility calling to tell me he was sick—or worse.

"Karen," Dad launched right in. "I just wanted to tell you I won at bingo this afternoon."

"What the hell is the matter with you? I've asked you a million times not to call during the day unless it's an emergency. Why can't you wait till the end of the day to tell me these things?"

"I'm sorry. I'm sorry. I won't do it again," he promised.

"Yeah, right," I shouted. "You're so selfish sometimes."

Later that day, I sobbed to a friend. "I'm no good. What kind of daughter treats her father that way? He's old. He's feeble. How can I yell at him like that? I'm becoming someone I don't like."

"Be gentle with yourself," she said. "He isn't an easy person to deal with and this is a difficult situation."

As I struggled in therapy to find a balance between caring for my father and maintaining my own life, I began to see a different man than I'd known before. Though at first, we treated each other much the same as he and my mother had, slowly I began to soften. Not just for his sake, but for mine. Paying closer attention to our conversations, I tried to separate the little girl inside from the adult I'd become. Little by little, I was able to stop the wounded child before she responded so the adult could take control. I began to talk to my father in ways I'd never been able to before. One day, after leaving the VA, he said, "You're causing so much trouble."

"You're the reason we had to come today, not me," I said. "I had plans to go to Santa Fe."

"No, no," he said. "I'm the trouble, not you." I suddenly realized Dad meant to say he was the one causing trouble, but it had come out backwards.

Dad cried. "I don't want to hurt you. You are my baby girl. I love you."

Wow. How long had I waited to hear that? I realized then that it would be my responsibility to discern what he was really trying to say and not always assume he was attacking me.

One afternoon I decided to read him an essay I'd written about losing custody of my son. I'd never shared my writing with him before. When I finished the story, he said, "You won't get that published."

145

I took a deep breath, holding back the sharp retort I would automatically have made and asked, "What do you mean, Dad?"

"You'll have to change the names. He'll come after you," he said, meaning my ex-husband.

"Did you like the story?"

"I didn't know any of this, Karen. You never told me. I would have killed him," Dad said.

"I know. So, what do you think?" I pushed for a compliment.

"You did a great job."

I'd never heard words like that before. Slowly, I began to feel my father's love. Nothing could make up for the Dad I had wanted and needed as a child, but finally we were becoming a loving father and daughter. At last I *wanted* to connect with him. So, in addition to talking twice a day and going on errands for him, Sunday became Dad Day.

* * *

July 2003

Gary and I love to travel. Each year we take one big trip, plus several smaller ones—usually family holiday trips or weekends at the cabin in Pecos. Now that Dad was so much a part of our daily life, we needed to take his needs into consideration as well. He had always talked about going to the Grand Canyon. He, too, loved to travel and Mom had refused to. We'd already taken him on several day trips around New Mexico: El Morro National Monument, Acoma Pueblo, and Bosque Del Apache. We were hesitant to venture as far as Arizona because it meant a long day's drive in the car as well as two nights in motels—maybe more. Gary and I discussed it at length and decided it was worth the effort.

The drive was hard on Dad. Bathroom stops took a half hour by the time we got the wheelchair out, helped him out of the car, walked him to the bathroom, waited while he did his business, and then settled him back in the vehicle. But once we arrived, watching this old man come alive as he took in the beauty and grandeur of the canyon was unforgettable. We stopped at a spot at the South Rim. Once again we maneuvered his wheelchair out of the trunk and walked him about three-quarters of a mile around the canyon, stopping at different viewpoints along the

146

way. At one particularly beautiful spot, Dad asked to rest. He watched two condors fly back and forth from one rock ridge to another. He was quiet, unusual for him.

After awhile he asked, "Do you think everything that's happened to me in the last few years is my meanness coming out?" He was referring to his skin condition.

"Is that what you think, Dad? Do you think you're mean?"

"Well, I was mean to your mother. But was I mean to you?"

I took a deep breath. "You said things that hurt me, but I don't think you intended to be mean, Dad. Like when I was seven and in that dance recital. You told me I looked like a whore because I had lipstick on."

Dad looked out at the great vistas of the canyon, then down at his lap. Several minutes went by and then he said, "I'm so sorry I wasn't able to give you what you needed as a child."

The lump of pain that had lived in my stomach for most of my life dissolved. At eighty-seven, he was saying the words I'd longed to hear for fifty years. It was a profound moment and I realized that I was forgiving my Dad just two years after my son had forgiven me.

With forgiveness, something shifted in my soul. I became grateful, rather than resentful, for this time with my father—and for having the opportunity to get to know him without the unhealthy dynamics between him and my mother or my childhood wounds getting in the way.

I got to be my father's keeper for two more years. The last trip we took with him was to San Antonio, so Dad could see The Alamo. He and Gary shared a love of westerns, and it was particularly moving for Dad to see the actual site of so many movies he had watched over the years. Dad took a bad spill on that trip, but was still very grateful we had taken him.

Less than one month later, he called on Christmas day to say he didn't feel well. At 2:00 am he called again and asked us to take him to the hospital. The doctors informed us he was having a massive heart attack. I spent the next few days at his bedside. He wasn't in a lot of pain, but couldn't talk much. David made plans to come out. On December 29, 2004, Gary left to pick David up at the airport. While I fed Dad his dinner, his eyes suddenly looked off to the right, staring into space. I ran for the nurses, who rushed into the room. Dad had left instructions not to resuscitate, so I quietly held his hand as we watched the squiggly green line on the monitor machine go straight. It was two months before his 90th birthday.

Shortly after we'd brought Dad home to New Mexico, I had changed Dad's pre-planned funeral arrangements. After the fiasco with my mother's ashes, I needed something more to honor my father's passing. Since the military had been such a proud part of my dad's life, I arranged for him to have a military service and to be buried in the National Cemetery in Santa Fe. We'd shown him the cemetery during one of our day trips and he'd gotten tears in his eyes. He loved the mountains of New Mexico, so it was fitting that his final resting place be in the state he'd come to regard as home with a military honor guard saluting him.

* * *

Chapter 12

Mother's Day

After Dad died, I put all my energy and attention into finishing my degree and finally, in December, 2005, I marched along with thousands of other graduates to receive my bachelor's degree with honors. All of my classes that last year were writing classes and several portions of this memoir were first drafted as assignments in Greg Martin's and Lisa Chavez's creative nonfiction classes as well as Jack Trujillo's and Marissa Clark's fiction classes. There I learned about dialogue, scene, vivid description, and the importance of details, among other techniques of the writing craft. One essay was published in "Best Student Essays, 2005" and another in UNM's literary magazine, Conceptions, as well as being nominated for a literary award. Additional essays were published in newspapers, magazines, and an anthology by Simon and Schuster. I am forever indebted to the professors in UNM's Creative Writing program for showing me how to "tell my story."

Graduation took place in early December and New Year's was fast approaching. I sat down to reflect on the past year and two resolutions emerged. The first was to become healthier in all areas, but mostly physical. I'd gained back half the forty-six pounds I'd lost a few years ago and was determined to not only take them off, but become more active as a lifestyle choice. The second resolution was to write my memoir, feeling more confident in how to tell my story.

For Christmas, Gary bought me a new retro bike, with high handle bars so my lower back wouldn't hurt from bending over. The bike had brakes on the foot pedals, just like a Schwinn I'd had as a kid. On January 2nd, we took the bike out for its first spin. Two happy miles later, I turned into the park behind our house and the next thing I knew I was feeling more pain than I thought possible. My bike slid on gravel, went out from under me, and somehow my ankle got caught, dislocated, and broke in three places—one bone in seven pieces.

"How bad is it?" I asked the emergency room physician, who walked in holding up my x-rays.

"Well, Karen, if you were a horse, we'd put you down," he said.

I turned to Gary.

"Aren't you glad I'm not a horse?" I asked him.

The doctor performed emergency surgery that very night. At home the next morning, I was completely helpless.

It is amazing how priorities shift as a result of such an instant upheaval. What became most important were the necessities like being fed, going to the bathroom, and finding a comfortable position to sit or lie in. It was as if a window into old age opened. Even though Gary brought the computer downstairs and set it up on the coffee table for me, I had no desire to write as I was unable to concentrate or focus for more than a few seconds.

I'm not sure why, but I felt as if the spirit I had worked so hard to heal had fractured along with my ankle. Depression descended once more. During the long, slow recovery—almost eight months until I could walk without much pain—I once again lost myself, entering that old familiar, safe, zoned-out place. Unable to move, I gained even more weight. And even when I could exercise, I was unsteady on my feet, and my ankle continuously hurt. Dancing was out of the question, and I wondered if, in fact, I'd ever dance again. I tried hard to find meaning from fracturing my ankle, but it eluded me.

One day, the UNM Continuing Education booklet arrived in the mail and I skimmed through it. A singing class was beginning in just a few weeks and another forgotten dream awoke. I wrote the check and sent it off immediately. If I couldn't dance, I'd sing—the other activity which had brought me comfort and joy when I'd been younger. I'd taught myself a few chords on the guitar I'd gotten for my 50ᵗʰ birthday and had spent many happy hours singing to my favorite songs. But a small voice whispered that singing lessons would help me.

The classes were held in a held in a studio called *The Singing Center*. There were nine or ten of us in the class and at first we sang as a group. The first time I was asked to sing solo in front of the class, I felt as if my vocal chords were frozen and I warbled off key. As long as I looked down at the floor, I could sing quietly on pitch, but if I became aware of the other students watching me, my voice cracked and I could barely sing above a whisper. As a result of listening to my intuition, I started private lessons, sensing an opportunity for deeper healing, even if I didn't know what or how.

"What you need," Diana, the instructor, said, "is to learn to breathe properly, sing in the appropriate voice register, and project your voice. Right now you sound like a little girl."

Unknowingly, Diana had hit the nail on the head. There was still a frozen little girl inside me, desperately yearning for love and attention; still wanting to "perform." The wounds from the dance recital when I was seven had never fully healed. Nor had I healed from being rejected by the sorority in high school. Somehow I'd linked being the center of attention and being myself with getting rejected. Singing offered a way for me to possibly shift that inaccurate perception. There was to be a student concert and I was determined to sing a solo.

At the same time, I entered a very different kind of therapy called Radix. It is body centered, designed to release repressed emotions. When I'd freeze up while standing at the microphone, I'd take that fear to Becky, my therapist, and she'd work with me until I was able to feel the hurt or anger or resentment and work it out of me.

I'm so grateful I listened to my intuition when I decided to take voice lessons. I had no idea at the time what the outcome would be—I'd just wanted to improve my voice. But by the time I performed in the concert, some six months after I'd started, I not only sang better, but felt more secure inside my own skin and had more confidence. Each time I get up and sing in front of our small group in class, it gets a little easier and I became more comfortable in front of others. To sing well, one must be grounded and centered; one must breathe fully and deeply in the belly; and one must project with authority into the audience. The combination of Radix therapy and the safe and loving environment Diana created during our lessons unleashed the sounds lying dormant in my body. I found my voice, literally and figuratively. And I might not have found this outlet had I not fractured my ankle and been unable to dance.

* * *

New York City, May 2007

My girlfriend Wendy and I decided to take a girl trip. She hadn't been to New York City in over thirty years, and I hadn't seen my son for several months. In addition, my ninety-one-year-old aunt was recovering from heart surgery, and I was afraid it might be my last chance to see her.

Our first night there, we watched David's comedy improvisation class perform. Upon greeting him, I experienced the same reactions I'd been having for years: I wished my son looked happy when he first saw me; I wanted more than monosyllabic responses. I still felt desperate for a deeper connection.

That Sunday, Wendy and I decided to attend a service of the world-renowned gospel choir at the Abyssinian Church in Harlem. Unfortunately, the line wound around the block, and we couldn't get in. Instead, we went around the corner to a different church. The service was not what we had expected, but since the minister was in the midst of speaking, we sat down to listen. She was discussing the trials and tribulations of human suffering—the pain and sorrow we carry around, as we desperately attempt to fix what is troubling us.

"But we can't," she said. "We must give these sorrows over to God."

I'd heard those words before, both in church and in the twelve-step programs, but I had forgotten. It was then I realized that I was still trying to fix what I felt was wrong between my son and me and that I needed to finally let that go. Wendy had told me the night before that she felt a great deal of tension between David and me—and it wasn't just coming from David. Shaken, I leaned over and whispered to Wendy that I needed to leave as soon as the minister was finished speaking.

Wendy looked at me as we strolled down 125th Street and said, "What happened in there?"

"Did you hear what she said about turning our problems over to God?" I asked.

Wendy nodded.

"Well, I had an epiphany about me and David. You were right the other night. I am tense around him. I'm always worried about his not talking and my talking too much, what more I can do to connect—it must drive him nuts."

Wendy didn't say anything, allowing me to rant for awhile.

"From now on, I am going to let go and let God. You can slap me upside the head if I start to talk about how miserable I am because of David," I told her. "I'm just going to be me. At this point, he is who he is and I am who I am. Sitting in that church, I really got that I can't make this relationship into something it's not.

We had several dinners and lunches with David during the week. But despite my epiphany, I couldn't quiet the anxiety I felt over not knowing if I would see him on Mother's Day, which was that coming Sunday. During one of the meals, I asked whether he was free that day. He said, "Sure, I can do that."

I thought back to the years I sat in my house, waiting for a phone call that never came. Long ago, I'd given up looking for a card in the mail. In the few years since David had been back in my life, he had called to wish me a happy Mother's Day, but it had been thirty years since I'd spent Mother's Day with my son.

It was an especially glorious spring day in New York—that wondrous window of time when winter has left and the summer heat and humidity have yet to arrive. Wendy wanted David and me to have this time alone, so she took off by herself. Since I wasn't meeting David for several hours, I took my journal to Central Park and sat on a bench, surrounded by deep purple, red, yellow, and white tulips. Dogwood trees bloomed white and pink and it seemed as if the entire city was out enjoying the cool spring morning.

Before I knew it, it was time to meet David at Pasha Turkish, across from our hotel. Arriving first, I waited on a plush, brocade chair in the lobby. When David came a few minutes later, he bent down to kiss me on the cheek.

"Happy Mother's Day," he said.

A seating hostess led us into the brightly lit dining room, with its

153

wine-colored walls and carpet. We sat across from one another and talked. David asked about my life and listened for my answers. He thoughtfully responded to questions and after learning about a fall I'd taken two days earlier, he acted with concern. We talked a bit about his plans for the future and his fears about ending up responsible for his father, who was unemployed and not doing much about his situation.

I told David to take advantage of my being in the city; that if he needed anything or wanted to do something he couldn't ordinarily afford, he should let me know.

"I need some new pants," he said shyly.

I was thrilled; I thought he'd only have time for lunch. We ended up spending the next few hours together. We bought two pairs of slacks and running shoes, and then it was time for us to part. David hailed a cab, gave me a scrumptious hug and helped me into the taxi. I turned around and saw him wave as he walked down the street.

Back in the hotel room, I filled Wendy in on our visit, puzzled by the ease and comfort I'd felt with David.

"I can't imagine that my letting go could create such a shift in our relationship, but something changed," I told her.

"You probably weren't as tense and anxious as you usually are," Wendy said. "Maybe David sensed that."

Just then the hotel phone rang. When I picked up, David said, "Hi, Mom. I'm downstairs. I've got something for you." I told him to come on up. Wendy and I looked at each other and shrugged.

David walked in with his bike helmet in one hand and a single red rose with white spray surrounding it in the other. I fumbled with the wrapping before finding a small card that said, "Happy Mother's Day. Thank you for spending this day with me. Love, David."

I turned to where David was seated on the bed next to Wendy. His eyes glowed with love.

"I can't stay," he said, "but I wanted you to have this." His smile lit up his face.

"You have no idea what this means to me, David," I said. "Thank you."

Wendy and I left New York the next morning. On the plane heading back to New Mexico, I told Wendy I didn't think Mother's Day would be a problem for me any longer—that though I knew this one loving

Mother's Day didn't mean everything would be the way I wanted it to be, I was finally letting go of trying to fix my relationship with my son. There was nothing more that needed fixing.

When I got home to New Mexico, Gary was waiting. Together we pressed the rose between wax paper and placed it between two heavy books. Several days later, I placed it on my dresser, where it serves as a reminder of my son's love and the pain we both endured before finding our way back to one another.

* * *

Chapter 13

Listening to the Whispers

G ary loves trains. To fulfill a lifelong dream of his, we took the train
through the Canadian Rockies. We flew to Vancouver, B.C. and
spent a day exploring this city, one of the most beautiful we'd ever seen.
The next morning, we boarded the Rocky Mountaineer. Because we had
purchased first class accommodations, we sat in a car with a glass dome,
affording views on either side of the train, as well as above. An elegant
breakfast was served and we sipped mimosas while passing 12,000 foot
snow-capped mountains and turquoise colored glacier-fed rivers. Winding
through the Rockies, the train travelled from Vancouver to Banff. From
there we rented a car and visited several national parks. On the way,
we saw osprey, eagles, black bears, and even a grizzly. When we arrived
at Lake Louise, the huge parking lot was empty and the path leading
through sparse woods towards the lake was devoid of people.

A light mist hovered over the water. Clouds dotted the surrounding
mountains and the glacier that nestles between two ridges at the far side
of the lake was not visible when we began our hike. Humbled by the
mystical beauty, I could not speak.

"We're lucky we're so early," Gary said. "The trail will be much busier
later in the morning."

As we made our way around the lake, we only passed a few people.
The far end is about half a mile away and by the time we got there, the
glacier was in full view. Gary wanted to continue hiking up the glacier,

156

but I chose to meander slowly back towards the Chateau (a famous lodge built by the railroad). I wanted some time alone to absorb the magic of the lake, which was tranquil, except for the occasional shimmer across the top as a duck dove for its breakfast. Gary disappeared behind the mountain ridge and I turned from the lake and started to walk. There was a bench about three feet in front of me and I strolled past it, hesitated for a moment, then turned back and sat down. No more than three seconds later, a boulder tumbled down the mountainside and landed right where I had been standing. Looking behind me, I saw a man scrambling down the mountain. He had bushwhacked off the trail, despite the many signs warning against this, dislodging plants, stones and the boulder that would have either killed or seriously maimed me if I hadn't chosen to sit down on the bench.

I sat shaking, not from the cold, but from the knowledge that I could have been killed, just like that. Why hadn't I? What made me turn back to the bench? Do things happen randomly or is there a God or some universal energy that guides our destiny? Some scientist friends of mine do not believe in God. Others maintain a sense of belief. My friends and I have had many late night discussions about religion, faith, spirituality, and divine order versus destiny. There are logical, reasonable explanations for both sides of the argument. And then there are the mysteries that cannot be explained.

My belief in Spirit keeps me grounded. It brings, as *The Book of Common Prayer* says, "The peace that passeth all understanding." I do believe in a universal energy that we can tap into—a connection to the Earth, the elements, to all living things. The twelve-step programs call it "God as we understand God," or "a power greater than ourselves." I discovered that calm energy as a child lighting Chanukah candles, then again saying the Lord's Prayer in the Episcopal Church. Later on, I found it in the New Thought Church and Earth-based spiritual traditions. Now I find it during my own prayer and meditation times as well as in Nature or by simply setting an intention to create sacred space and opening myself up to that loving energy. And I believe I was connected to it that day on Lake Louise.

Gary Zukav in *Seat of the Soul* talks about authentic power, which is very different from the power most people search for—a certain amount of money, a degree of achievement in a profession, having a healthy family.

He says authentic power is when our actions come from the heart; when our personality is aligned with our soul and what we do in our life is about serving the needs of the soul, not seeking external power. He says it much better than I can, but what he's saying is very much what I've tried to do with my life in terms of work, career and money. I just didn't have words for what I was doing. My soul was restless and unhappy until I let go and started writing. But it took me thirty years to pay attention and attempt to do what my heart was telling me to do. What comes up now by way of obstacles are what Zukav calls "holy moments"—opportunities to choose differently from what you have in the past. I used to call them blocks and allowed myself to get stopped by them. Now I search for the lesson or meaning that might be trying to get through to me, such as going back to school or taking singing lessons.

Sometimes I feel as if I am being tested. How strong is my will and determination? How committed am I? With this book, I knew I wouldn't let anything stand in the way of completing it. It had to come out of me, whether it got published or not. If you are reading this, I was successful in ways I didn't dream of while writing the book. As I read through my journal entries over the past twenty years, writing was always there, but as had been my habit, I just wasn't listening. Fortunately, I have a husband who can support me financially while I write, but I would have needed to find a way to write anyway, or my soul would continue to feel restless and sad.

Somewhere during my journey, I began to realize that many of my desires were a spiritual quest for knowing God's love. Food, sex, and people were all ways I tried to fill the void I felt. As I moved further along the spiritual path, that void began to fill with Spirit.

But believing in Spirit and acknowledging the whispers are separate issues. When Spirit speaks to me, sometimes I listen. But sometimes I don't. I could just as easily have chosen to keep walking that day at Lake Louise. Or I could have decided not to move to Portland to escape my pain. Or I might have convinced myself life wasn't worth living anymore out there in the Mojave Desert. Was I truly being guided, or is life just a crap shoot? Does everything happen exactly as it is supposed to? Perhaps nobody really knows. What I do know is that when I began to listen to what I've come to know as the voice of wisdom, my broken spirit started to mend. Self-hated no longer resides in my psyche. Where there was hate, there is now compassion for myself and respect for all the work I did to heal. I needed to grieve the losses, accept the choices and decisions I made, honor the regrets and learn to get quiet and pray to reach the degree of comfort I now have with myself. This is my life's work. To heal the hurts, reduce the amount of time I am in emotional and/or psychological pain, and learn to love unconditionally—others as well as myself. It continues. I am a work in progress.

My weight continues to fluctuate—right now I'm on a downswing. The twelve-step programs have a slogan: The definition of insanity is doing the same thing over and over and expecting a different result. According to that definition, when it came to my weight, I was insane. Over the years, I counted points on Weight Watchers, ate frozen Jenny Craig food, worked out at Inches Away, guzzled Slim Fasts, slipped into trances in hypnotherapy, charged my body with Energy Tapping, yelled my emotions in Radix, and discovered my inner child in traditional talk therapy. Each time, I reached my goal weight, then proceeded to gain all or most of the weight back. So two years ago, when an orthopedic surgeon told me I needed knee surgery but wouldn't operate until I lost weight, something snapped. I knew I had to do things differently.

For months after the surgeon's pronouncement I resisted, complained, and procrastinated, but eventually reached acceptance. I needed a plan. I wasn't comfortable in gyms where young people with buff bodies strutted their stuff. I am not, nor have I ever been inclined to jog or play sports. If I attempt something athletic like swimming or biking, invariably I break a bone or strain a muscle. I'd already broken one ankle—I couldn't afford to break anything else.

Instead, I found a gym filled mostly with folks on oxygen and who use walkers to get around. At fifty-nine, I was one of the youngest members. Exercise physiologists gave me a workout structure based on my personal history and physical abilities so I wouldn't hurt myself or try to do too much too fast. The staff nutritionist taught me how to eat healthily without being obsessed.

I didn't understand this at the time, but what I came up with was a way to become conscious about my body and food. Eckhart Tolle, in *A New Earth*, says that humans carry an accumulation of old emotional pain, which he calls "the pain-body." He goes on to say that the "pain-body" thrives on negativity, using emotionally painful experiences as food. No

159

wonder I couldn't sustain weight loss. My "pain-body" craved misery. Unless I learned to recognize when my "pain-body" became activated, it would continue to seek what it knew best—pain and suffering.

I decided to weigh myself every day. In previous endeavors, this led to obsession and acute, daily frustration with results (or lack thereof). This time, however, my goal was to learn about and understand my body—to see what factors influenced my weight. I learned not to identify with what I saw on the scale. When I caught myself at the labeling game: "good" if I lost a pound; "bad" if I didn't, I did what Tolle advises—accept "what is."

Everyone's body is different, and I found what works for mine: I am hypoglycemic, but did not understand how that was affected by nutrition. I must eat a minimum of three starch servings per day (i.e. one slice of bread; ½ cup of whole wheat pasta). Otherwise, I get light-headed and quite irritable. Drinking enough fluids was important as well—I tend to retain water. Adding fruit and vegetables into my diet was hard, but crucial. I switched from products with white flour to whole grain pastas and breads. Finally, I needed to start taking probiotic supplements to normalize my body's digestive system. Irregularity influences body weight.

Most importantly, I became aware of and familiar with the negative self-talk constantly running through my head. It was a challenge to remain alert enough to recognize the voice of "the pain-body" and not react in the old, insane ways. But as this process unfolded, my attitudes began to shift and I found myself making different choices. What emerged were eight predominant ways my "pain-body" tried to sabotage my weight loss. Tolle teaches us not to reject or resist our negative emotions, but to acknowledge their existence. Awareness and acceptance must come before actions if lasting changes are to occur. These are the internal dialogues from my "pain-body, followed by the positive way I reframed them:

1. *Don't get on the scale. Then you can pretend you're not gaining the weight back.*
   The scale is my friend and keeps me honest. If my weight begins to creep up, I can stop it at five pounds, rather than thirty.

2. *Wear only clothing with elastic waists so you can pretend your clothes still fit.*
   If that zipper is a little snug, it's time to take inventory. I need to get on the scale and find out how much damage I've done and take corrective action immediately.

3. *Don't keep track of what you are eating each day so you can tell yourself you stayed within your food plan.*
   Pay close attention to food choices and how my body feels before, during and after eating. This is especially important after I have reached my goal weight.

4. *When you measure your portion sizes, it is okay to add a little bit here and there. It really won't make a difference.*
   It really does make a difference. A little bit here, a little bit there adds up to a lot over time.

5. *Once you reach your goal weight, you do not have to watch yourself that closely. Like magic, your weight will remain stable.*
   I have had a weight problem my whole adult life. It won't go away just because I lost weight and achieved my goal. I have to remain watchful and stick to my new way of eating. I have to remain conscious and awake.

6. *It's okay to allow your mood to affect your decisions about food. It's really okay if you are angry, depressed, sad, upset or happy and feel like eating. Go ahead and do it. You deserve to make yourself feel better or celebrate something.*
   Emotional eating is not okay. It is a momentary "fix" of the mood problem, but creates a much larger, longer-lasting problem—being overweight. I need to find other ways to soothe and comfort myself when my emotions flare up.

7. *When your friends or family members tell you it is okay to eat what you want just this once, listen to them. They know better than you do what is best for you.*
   No one knows better than me what is good for me. Find

161

ways to gently explain to my friends and family that I am working hard to eat healthily and it is important that I stick to my plan.

8. *Even if you are feeling full, if that dish tastes better than anything you've ever tasted, it's okay to finish it. Never leave food on a plate, especially at a restaurant. After all, you paid for it, you better finish it.* **Despite the fact that there are people starving, it really is okay for me to leave food on my plate. I ask for a doggie bag at the beginning of the meal, and put half my meal into it. If I want dessert, I share it with someone. If no one wants to share and I can't let go of the craving, I order what I want, take a few bites, and either leave the rest or bring it home.**

These are the most frequent "pain-body" voices in my head. As I become more alert, I notice others. Catching them in the moment, rather than after I've already behaved unconsciously is vital not only to my weight loss success, but to a peaceful life as well. I've lost and gained thirty-plus pounds four or five times in my adult life. Since the wakeup call from the surgeon and beginning this new way of approaching weight, I have lost thirty-six pounds. I don't have a crystal ball to know whether I will keep it off this time. What I do know is my attitude towards and my relationship with food has changed. I no longer diet. I follow the nutritionist's guidelines as well as I can. And I've quit the gym, preferring to sweat to the oldies with Richard Simmons in the quiet and solitude of my own living room.

The most significant change, however, is being aware of my body and how it feels. The energy and intensity I had around eating has lifted and the negative voices, although still there, are much quieter and show up much less frequently. Then, too, there is a new voice that comes in the stillness of being awake. If I listen carefully, it whispers, *I'm full*, and I stop eating, or *you don't really want those potatoes—you want salad instead.* I don't always pay attention and then the scale reflects the consequences. But more and more, I am present inside my own skin—and that has made me feel quite sane regarding eating.

Henry Thoreau said "The mass of men live lives of quiet desperation." The question is, do we have to continue to do so? Some people may be

162

content with their lives just as they are. Others, like me, want more.

It's a little over nine years since I quit my job to figure out what was next in my life. Writing this book pulled at my guts, made me cry, made me doubt my writing ability and myself. It made me work at accepting Gary's gift of support. Sometimes it hurt. Other times it felt great. One day it was difficult, the next time words flowed easily through me. Spirit was most definitely guiding me each step of the way. Writing brought pieces of the puzzle of my life together for me, synthesizing the pain and agony and the healing work inside my soul. And when I doubted yet again, a friend handed me Eckhart Tolle's book, *A New Earth*, which talks about life purpose and in it, Tolle says our purpose is to awaken. An epiphany occurred when I realized that writing has been my main avenue to awaken my consciousness, and therefore, my purpose is to write.

I fit inside my own skin now, aware of my body and all its sensations. In any given moment, I am aware of what I am feeling and am capable of expressing myself clearly and honestly. I love and feel loved by family and friends. More lessons are in store for me, I know, and more pain, more happiness and more experiences as I live my life. But I also know that I can manage it by staying awake, aware and focused, continuing my daily prayer and meditation, and following the path of my heart. This is the "work" all the spiritual masters tell us we need to do to move forward on the spiritual path. It is the work Eckhart Tolle refers to as "awakening."

The whispers of Spirit have always been with me. I simply had to wake up in order to listen. My sense of God, spirituality and the universe has expanded to include everything. I believe in Judaism. I believe in Christianity. I believe in New Thought. I believe in Native American Spirituality. I believe in the Goddess religion. I believe in Buddhism. I believe in Hinduism. Have I left anything out? If I did, please include it. I needed to awaken and find a connection to a source of wisdom and energy outside of myself and to find my own way to that source. And I needed to learn that my own inner wisdom is connected to Spirit. My hope is that all of us can find our own way and walk that path with love in our hearts—for ourselves as well as for the rest of us on this planet some call Mother Earth—and to keep listening for the whispers.

- End -

About the Author

Karen Walker is a writer who has published essays in newspapers and magazines, as well as in an anthology series. After a 30+ year career in marketing and public relations, she went back to college to complete a Bachelor's degree and graduated Summa Cum Laude in 2005 from the University of New Mexico's University Studies program with a major emphasis in Creative Writing. She lives in Albuquerque, New Mexico with her husband, Gary, and their dog, Buddy.

To contact Karen Walker, please visit her website at
www.followingthewhispers.com